The Prairie Garden

70 Native Plants You Can Grow
in Town or Country

J. Robert Smith
with Beatrice S. Smith

The University of Wisconsin Press

Published 1980

The University of Wisconsin Press
114 North Murray Street
Madison, Wisconsin 53715

The University of Wisconsin Press, Ltd.
1 Gower Street
London WC1E 6HA, England

First printing

Printed in the United States of America

For LC CIP Information see the colophon

ISBN 0-299-08300-4 cloth; 0-299-08304-7 paperback

Contents

Acknowledgments

Line drawings of individual species by Patricia Mueller.

Photographs on pages 33–48 by Richard Williamson, with the following exceptions:

Virginia Kline, *Eryngium yuccifolium*, p. 37.

Lorrie Otto, *Silphium perfoliatum*, p. 43.

B. W. Trimm, *Hudsonia tomentosa*, p. 39, and *Carex pensylvanica*, p. 48.

Richard R. Gunderson, Rockford, IL, landscape (center), p. 48; courtesy of Windrift Prairie Shop and Nursery, Dot and Doug Wade, Oregon, IL.

Ruth Wynn, *Baptisia leucantha*, p. 35.

Cost Comparison Chart, p. 208, courtesy of Prairie Restorations, Inc., Wayzata, MN.

Map of locations of prairies, p. 211, courtesy of the National Geographic Society, Washington, D.C. Redrawn for this book by the University of Wisconsin-Madison Cartographic Laboratory.

Preface

What exactly, I've been asked, are prairie plants?

Prairie plants are native grasses and forbs (flowering herbs) that grow on a prairie.

What is a prairie?

Some people say a prairie is a state of mind. Scientists believe it is close to being the most complex, yet the most balanced ecosystem on earth. The word *prairie*, meaning meadow, was the name French explorers called the vast treeless landscape they found stretched throughout middle America. Dominated by grasses, this landscape falls roughly into three area groups. West in the high dry plains sloping from the Rocky Mountains eastward is the short-grass prairie. As rainfall increases, the mid-grass prairie emerges. Covering parts of North and South Dakota, Nebraska, Oklahoma, Kansas, Texas, Missouri, Iowa, and extending into Minnesota, Wisconsin, Illinois, Indiana, and Ohio is the tall-grass, or true, prairie.

The prairie plants discussed in this book are natives of the tall-grass prairie.

The tall-grass prairie may be dry, mesic, or wet, with gradations between.

The dry prairies have shallow dry soils and are found on sand and on limestone areas. To me, those on the limestone areas, sometimes called goat prairies, are the most spectacular.

Mesic prairies are the ones the North American settlers plowed so eagerly. They have good drainage and deep organic soil. Plants are generally higher, coarser, and heavier than those on dry prairies.

Wet prairies have organic soil that drains poorly, and often are found blending with sedge meadows, cattail marshes, and the more alkaline fens.

Many prairie plants are found on mesic prairies; fewer, on dry and on moist. Some can be found on all three prairies. Still others are found on two of the three. Seventy of these kinds of prairie plant species are discussed in this book.

I have included only those plants with which I have had personal experience. Propagation methods described are practical, proven methods developed over a period of 14 years, including 10 years of operating Prairie Nursery, at Westfield, Wisconsin, where we grow prairie seeds and plants commercially.

I am not a botanist or a plant ecologist. My basic training was in forestry and wildlife management. However, I have been a gardener as long as I can remember and have had agricultural experience both in Wisconsin and in California.

This book has been prepared as an aid to beginners interested in using prairie plants for landscaping small areas and to others wanting to establish or improve large prairie areas. It will, I hope, be a partial answer to a question I frequently receive in the mail, asking for "all the information you have on the propagation of prairie plants."

Although the information contained herein is largely the result of trial and error, no book can be wholly original. Before anyone can practice or preach prairie propagation, he must read what others have practiced and preached. I have attempted to do so, and I have included a list of suggested reading. To those authors and to those who have shared ideas with me, I owe a great deal. I am especially indebted to Philip B. Whitford, who read this manuscript and gave freely of his expertise. A pioneer in prairie plant ecology, he is Chairman of the Department of Botany, University of Wisconsin-Milwaukee.

January 1980   J. ROBERT SMITH

The Prairie Garden

1
An Introduction

My interest in prairies goes back to the 1930s when as a boy I hunted sharptail grouse on the Douglas County barrens of northern Wisconsin. Barrens are similar to prairies in many ways and contain many of the same plants, often dwarfed by desertlike conditions in summer. In fall, vast open spaces of grass speckled with asters and goldenrod reach to the horizon, broken only by scattered clumps of oak, jack pine, and aspen. I remember the great sense of freedom the space gave me, just me, with my setter by my side, my single-barreled 16-gauge shotgun over my shoulder, and an apple in my pocket. The next time I hunted there the area had changed considerably. So had I. The barrens had been planted to jack pine. I nearly wore myself out walking across the furrows. The last time I was there rows of pine trees stood 20 feet tall. The barrens were gone. I still feel the loss.

My interest in prairies was further stimulated when as a Department of Natural Resources employee I was involved administratively in the statewide acquisition and management of fish and game areas. Some of the first prescribed burning on a large scale was in the Crex Meadow Conservation Area in Burnett County in northwestern Wisconsin to improve waterfowl and prairie grouse range. Under the direction of Norman Stone, District Game Manager, and Burton Dahlburg, Area Supervisor, a dense forest of 20- to 30-year-old oak and jack pine was burned in the spring of 1957. To everyone's surprise, including that of Professor John T. Curtis of the University of Wisconsin Botany Department, examination of the Area in July 1957 revealed more than 70 species of prairie plants, some in bloom.

Stone reported that on further study of the Area and of unburned adjacent sites, botanists concluded that the prairie plants were present in dwarfed or semidormant form and responded immediately to sunlight when fire removed the shade. It was an exciting time for botanists and for the rest of us.

My relationship with prairies intensified in 1959, the year my family bought a 154-acre farm in Marquette County in central Wisconsin. At that time the property was in a state of disrepair. The house was a broken-down fishing shanty. The soil had not been tilled for many years. Cattle meandered at will through the neglected pastures and in and out of the jack pine and oak, drinking water from the trout stream, and ruining the bank cover. The spring-fed pond was used as a dump. Wind swept across the sand. The terrain, molded by ancient, earth-grinding glaciers, was flat; there were no pretty ridges, no green valleys. But not far from the house was a long-abandoned family garden on a gentle north slope. A few thousand years ago it probably had been a shallow sedge marsh. It contained a plentiful amount of organic matter, augmented over the years by frequent applications of manure. Southward, the organic matter gradually diminished to dry sand. Thus, at least in sand country terms, I had at my fingertips moist, mesic, and dry prairie soil. In addition, scattered throughout the acreage were many native plants that included a variety of prairie species.

Orange-red butterfly weed was the first prairie plant to catch my eye that year of 1959. I noticed it during the long walks I took with my wife Bea and our two then-young sons. One sturdy butterfly weed plant was growing in the corner of a neglected field made up mostly of cool-season grasses. The brilliance of that butterfly weed could be seen a quarter mile away. I was impressed, but there were other jobs demanding attention. The house had to be made habitable. A hundred years of junk had to be removed from the pond. A moving sandblow had to be tied down. Fences had to be built. A vegetable garden had to be prepared. Not until 1966 was I able to return to my butterfly weed.

In 1966, I also, happened upon Kenfield's *The Wild Gardener in the Wild Landscape* (see Suggested Reading). Kenfield took long walks as I did, and to make them more interesting established wild and domestic flowering plants at intervals throughout his property. I questioned his methods; still, it was an intriguing idea. Why couldn't I have clumps of butterfly weed growing where I wanted them?

4

In September and October of 1966 I collected seed from my butterfly weed just as the pods were beginning to burst. I put the seed into a pail and stored it in the barn loft, a safe, dry place. The following spring I sowed the seed. In 10 days it was up. By fall, there were carrotlike roots 4 to 5 inches long, ideal for transplanting wherever I chose. The procedure seemed simple.

Lupine was the next prairie plant to capture my attention. The lupine plants on the farm property were blue-blossomed, beautiful, hardy, and plentiful. But most of them were along the roadside where they were mowed down by the county weed-cutter. They deserved better. There was another stand in an area overrun by jack pine and oak. The plants were only 4 to 10 inches high with no bloom. I longed to bring them sunlight, but burning was out of the question. Why couldn't I transplant the doomed and the dwarfed?

I tried. To my amazement, transplanting wild lupine was impossible. The long white brittle root was too big to move successfully. Seed seemed to be the answer. Scrounging on my hands and knees, I found a few seeds scattered on the ground. I planted them, watered them, protected them; but no seeds germinated. Why not?

The seed had to be fresh, I decided. The next summer I watched an old stand of lupine carefully, saw the pods turn yellow, then black. Finally on a hot July morning the dried pods began twisting and bursting, throwing seeds up to 15 feet. Quickly, I scrambled on all fours and picked up the fresh seed that had fallen, then took it back and sowed it on a site I had prepared.

The seeds sprouted nicely, including a few I accidentally dropped on top of the soil. But it was July, a very dry July, and disaster struck. All my young lupine seedlings shriveled and died. Obviously, lupine seed must be sown in April or May in Wisconsin to take advantage of the cool, rainy season. My loss of seedlings was a hard lesson, but it set me thinking.

Fresh, still-soft lupine seeds taken directly from the pod germinated immediately. In fact, with exceptionally favorable moisture conditions they germinate on top of the soil. Those first lupine seeds I'd tried had already developed a tough seedcoat impervious to water. That's why they had not germinated. But there was hope for them. Lupine, I knew, belongs to the legume family. I was enough of a farmer to know that all domestic legumes require scarification, a scratching of the seedcoat to admit moisture. This was something I could try with the lupine seeds the following spring. But it was fall. What could I do?

Looking over the old lupine stand again, I found a few hard, dried seeds lying about just as I had before. And as before, their coats were too hard to permit moisture to enter. Germination would take place naturally the next spring after the seeds had softened and dampened. Could I imitate nature?

I took the dried, hard lupine seeds, sowed half of them ¾ inch deep in the vegetable garden near the house. In early March of the following year, I scarified the remainder of the seed, dampened it, and put it in the refrigerator.

Unfortunately, that was a busy spring. Four weeks passed. By the time I returned to the farm, the lupine seed in the refrigerator had sprouted and become moldy, and was no longer fit to plant. The seed in the garden was up and doing well, but it was too big to transplant. All in all, there was little to show for 2 years of effort. But at least I knew that dry lupine seed, scarified, dampened, and stored in a refrigerator, would germinate. And so would fall-planted lupine seed.

The next year I tried again, and was rewarded with a fine stand. It wasn't easy to establish. I always had drought to fight. But once established, my lupine plants increased in density and number and eventually their blue blossoms were as delightful to behold as I had imagined they would be.

With the lupine case solved, I took on spiderwort. Not being a member of the legume family, it could not be treated like one. I first sowed dry spiderwort seed in the spring of 1969, hoping it might be this easy. It wasn't; nothing came up.

The next April I planted early potatoes in the same general area. In June, while hoeing the potatoes, I noticed a thin wavy line of seedlings. Spiderwort seedlings? I knew the seeds of some conifers were subjected to damp cold to break their dormancy. Had overwintering in the soil "turned on" the spiderwort seed? And what about that first butterfly weed seed, my first success? By storing it in the cold dry barn loft, had I accidentally subjected it to the treatment it required to germinate?

At that point I did what I should have done in the beginning. I went to the University of Wisconsin Arboretum and talked with Jim Zimmerman and other natural scientists. Additional information came from further reading and conversations. The more I learned, the more enthusiastic I became, and the more I experimented.

One of the great thrills was the day I discovered how to induce New Jersey tea to germinate. So far as I knew, no one had been entirely successful. One evening while paging through Clyde Robin's catalog (see Suggested Reading), I happened on this statement regarding a western species of *Ceanothus*: "To germinate *Ceanothus*, pour boiling water over seeds and allow to cool." *Ceanothus* was the same genus as New Jersey tea. Would it work? It would, and the water didn't have to be boiling, I discovered. Water at 135° F worked fine for me and still does.

Throughout the years what has impressed me most about prairie plants, in addition to their beauty and complexity, is their persistence.

I have seen showy goldenrod sow itself in the mowed section of our lawn, and survive season after season of clipping. I have seen black-eyed susan bloom in the graveled ramp that leads to our barn loft, and manage to keep its head up despite being run over by tractor wheels some 50 to 100 times. The first butterfly weed plant I spotted in 1959 has been blooming every year, except one. For some reason it disappeared in 1969, but returned in 1970, flourished in the following years, and now looks as if it might live forever.

Then there's incredible leadplant. In April 1974 I pruned a bundle of 2-year-old leadplant, leaving roots 6 to 8 inches long, and placed the roots in a heeling bed. Most of the plants were sold that spring, but a few remained with their tips 5 or 6 inches underground. The area was cultivated regularly that summer and the following spring. Prairie smoke was transplanted into the area, and the area irrigated. Up came the leadplant. In fact, the leadplant appeared each year thereafter despite cultivation. In July 1979 I dug up what I thought to be a group of four or five plants. It turned out to be one plant with six 6-inch green shoots with leaves. The old pruning cuts were still visible where the root tip had been cut off. From this cut was a 10-inch broken root at a right angle from the stem. There were four other short lateral roots. And from the old bud was a new 5-inch leader to the soil surface.

Prairie plants have many ways of fighting destruction. They resist fire and drought the same way they resist the shovel, by an extensive root system. They resist winter weather through hardening. They resist water loss through specialization of their aboveground parts. They resist competition by cooperating with companion plants and closing out intruders. They take advantage of wind, birds, and insects. They must have long hours of sunshine to survive, but, relatively speaking, little else. Once established, prairie plants require no covering, no pruning, no spraying, and most important, no irrigating, thus saving prairie gardeners hundreds of dollars in maintenance costs. (See Cost Comparison Chart.) In fact, with ever-decreasing energy sources, the only ornamental plant of the future may well be the hardy native that requires no artificial watering.

However, simply sitting back and letting nature take its course is not the same as establishing a sod of prairie grasses and forbs. A prairie landscape will take a minimum of 3 or 4 years to establish and as much or more time and effort as the most cultivated lawn and garden.

My suggestions, learned the hard way, may help. With prairie gardening as with all gardening there is more to success than just following the rules. Conditions differ. Weather changes. Prairie plants are complex and highly variable organisms. The unforseen often happens. So consider my suggestions and mix them with your own experiences, hunches, and common sense.

2
Planning and Preparation

Planning

After deciding that you are willing to work at establishing a prairie area, take a walk around your property and see if there is a spot suited to growing prairie plants. The site must have from 70 to 100 percent sunlight.

Before planting anything, you should have an overall plan. Even if you toss it aside later, a plan will serve as a guide.

Get a sheet of graph paper and mark the boundaries of the site, scaling it as accurately as possible. Mark the location of existing buildings, walks, driveways; and indicate soil types, exposure, slopes. Now you have a bird's-eye-view of the problems to be solved. At this point you may throw up your hands and decide to call a landscape architect or your local nursery. However, if you decide to go ahead on your own, here are some suggestions:

1. Decide how you intend to use your prairie. Is it a place to stroll? Then you will need paths. Is it for wildlife? Then you may want tall grasses. Is it for many purposes? Then diversify.

2. Match plants to soil, slope, and exposure.

3. Fit the size of the plants to the size of the area. Proper balance and proportion are important in any good design. Keep tall plants to the edges and back of and away from buildings.

4. Place plants as nature might; no regular rows, no sharp corners, and no little square patches here and there. Free-flowing curves, turns, twists, and swoops; that's nature's way.

5. Try for continuous color throughout the growing season. (See index of color and flowering time.)

6. Allow one species to dominate, then blend to another. A species should be thick enough to be felt, even though it might mean planting fewer varieties. Give the more aggresive species competition.

7. Remember that a prairie is a grassland, with perhaps 50 to 85 percent of the area taken up by grasses.

8. Introduce species into natural habitats. Keep exceptions to a minimum.

9. Make use of existing features, such as house, shed, rocks, fences, walls, ponds, slopes, and swales.

10. On large areas, leave space for a firebreak.

11. Whatever the size of your site, when you begin a prairie landscape it is wise to "think small." This is especially true if you lack time, energy, experience, help, and/or proper equipment. Starting on a modest scale gives you time to learn about the plants and how they adapt to your site. It also leaves room to expand, using your own seed and transplants.

Site Preparation

The site should be chosen at least by August of the year before you sow a single seed. This will provide time to get rid of undesirable plants over part of two growing seasons. Undesirable plants, plants which successfully compete with prairie plants and spoil the character of the prairie, are here called weeds. The most persistent are perennial cool-season grasses, such as quack, brome, and bluegrass. Their rhizomes and roots must be destroyed.

Rhizomes are killed when exposed to sun and to frost. In Wisconsin, if you start working on them in July or August, continue at intervals into November, and finish the following April and early May, the site should be ready to plant by June 1.

On small areas undesirable competitive plants can be dug by hand, and their rhizomes and roots removed. It also may be feasible to cover the area with black plastic, anchored so that it won't blow with the wind. However, any area small enough to be covered with plastic usually is small enough to hand cultivate—and the results are much more satisfactory.

For a large area you need large equipment. First it must be plowed, then periodically cultivated with a rototiller or a spring-tooth harrow. A disk can be used, but it does not work the rhizomes to the surface of the soil where they must be if they are to be destroyed. As with small areas, repeated cultivation is necessary in summer, fall, and spring before planting begins.

Herbicides

Although my experience with herbicides is limited, you may wish to consider their use. If so, follow, exactly, the directions on a label. If, for instance, a label states, "one quart of 'Round-Up' per acre," that is exactly what you must use. Most gardeners are not equipped for precision spraying. If herbicides are used on large areas, they should be applied with appropriate equipment by an experienced operator.

On large areas or small, most herbicides will kill only those plants that are actively growing when the herbicide is applied. Dormant rhizomes will continue to live, so some cultivation may still be necessary. In addition, although herbicides, supposedly, rootkill only the plants they touch, their use does create some doubt in one's mind if a species does not take hold as it should. There is certainly a possibility that herbicide residues inhibit new prairie seedlings, particularly if herbicides are applied in excess of recommended amounts.

Most prairie enthusiasts are antiherbicide; some violently so. Nevertheless, there are managers responsible for natural vegetation on large areas who favor the careful use of herbicides to discourage undesirable plants.

Soil

Prairie plants grow on a variety of soils. In Wisconsin, for instance, prairie plants originally were found on the most fertile agricultural soils in the state, on the infertile sand areas, and on rocky bluffs and hillsides.

Mesic and dry prairie plants do well in loose soils with good drainage, and will tolerate a wide range of soil fertility and acidity. Low-fertility sites improve the competitive position of prairie plants against annual weeds and domestic grasses. High fertility will cause the plants to grow large and coarse, thus making them undesirable in small areas.

If possible, choose a site with sandy soil and good drainage. The advantages of sandy soil compared to other soil types include easy site preparation, weed control, and transplanting. The surface soil dries quickly, so that it can be worked after a rain. However, sand erodes easily and steep slopes should be avoided.

The ultimate question, and another reason for starting small, is how will the plants you select do on your soil?

Topography

What of the topography of your site? The landslope determines only surface drainage. Soil drainage depends on porosity of sub-soil. If there are pools of water standing 3 or 4 hours after a heavy rainfall, you can be sure drainage is poor. If so, you will either have to settle for wet prairie plants or do something to change the soil.

If cost and labor are no problem, change the soil by mixing in sand. The sand you want is not what you get from the average sand and gravel company. That is much too coarse. The sand you want is field sand, the kind that supports ground cover. A visit to your local nursery can be helpful.

What if your site has slopes and swales, high dry places, and a bit of a bog? Variations in topography are desirable. They furnish opportunities to use a wide range of prairie species. If, for example, your site has a swale where rain collects for a short time, you might introduce a few bottle gentian or culversroot. Or if your mesic site has a dry gravel hill, you might add crushed limestone and use it for dry prairie species.

You might even want to improve on nature and make a few topographical adjustments of your own. Consider the Japanese garden, where valleys are dug, bridges built, sand hauled, rocks moved, and water introduced. Even waterfalls are constructed to produce a variety of pleasing musical notes. No effort is spared. For lesser mortals wanting only to vary their prairie area, all you need is a shovel and a rake.

With rake or shovel, accentuate a swale by removing a few inches of soil and use the soil to increase the degree of a slope. Then rake it smooth. On large areas a grader will do the job.

Be prepared for adjustments—a planter's way may not always be a plant's way. A gentian, for instance, may not take to your hand-created wet habitat. If not, give up and try a different species. What you want are no-care hardy natives, not time-consuming invalids. Indeed, prairie plants, for the most part, do not need coddling. Theirs is a no-nonsense world with its own rules.

3
Collecting and Processing Seed

Collecting Seed

Collecting and preparing prairie seed is the first step in the creation of a prairie landscape whatever its size or purpose.

You can either buy seed from a nursery (see list of sources), or you can gather your own supply. Whichever way you choose, using seed from sources as close to your site as possible is the best way to ensure that your prairie plants are those adapted to the soil and climate of your locality.

If you live in an area where prairie plants were present originally, it is likely that remnants remain. Look along railroad and highway right-of-ways, on back roads, steep or rocky hills, abandoned farm fields. Always ask permission before collecting on private property, even if it belongs to a friend. Do not collect on designated natural areas. Do not clean out any patch completely, leave enough for reseeding. And do not molest endangered species. No species listed in this work, is, endangered or threatened in Wisconsin at present. If you live in another state, check with your state Department of Natural Resources.

If you decide to collect your own seeds, the first step is to scout likely sources during bloom and mark them on a map. Use inconspicuous ties or stakes or photograph the area to aid in relocating the plants. Spotting blooming plants and collecting their seeds will take you onto highways and byways from April into November in Wisconsin. (See descriptions of individual species for times.)

Collected seeds can be put into paper bags; plastic bags tend to hold moisture. Plastic pails work fine; I fasten one to my belt so I can pick with both hands.

Seed must be picked when ripe or just before. Ripeness can be determined by dryness of the seed and surrounding tissue. Use the dates for seed collection in the descriptions of individual species as a guide. Do not depend on them entirely. Seeds can vary widely by area and by year. Collect additional seed in good years—years with adequate rainfall. Always, if you can, pick more seed than you think you will need; you may have to replant. It pays to pick seed with as little foreign material in it as possible.

About half of the species to be discussed here have seedheads, seeds, or both, that drop to the ground. These seeds must be picked before they drop.

Some species have seeds that are carried by the wind: *Liatris* species, pasque flower, goldenrod, butterfly weed, marsh milkweed, asters, little bluestem. These seeds must be picked before the wind disperses them.

Some species have seedheads that explode: prairie phlox, flowering spurge, lupine, birdsfoot violet. The seeds from these types of plants must be picked early and allowed to explode where they can be contained.

Other species have multiple flowering heads with individual flowers blooming singly, with seeds dropping before all flowers have bloomed. Spiderwort is an example. Pick the whole heads and place them on ¼ inch screen over a matching box. As the seedheads dry, the seeds drop through the screen. They should be rolled around daily. Use the same method for bergamot and blackeyed susan.

Drying Seed

After seeds are picked, they should be spread thinly on screening and allowed to become thoroughly dry to prevent mold. Ordinary window screens will do. If the screens can be placed in the sun, so much the better. (Caution: Do not let seeds get over 100° F or leave them outdoors overnight. Plumed or very light seeds must be protected from wind.)

In damp fall weather, drying large amounts of seed can be a slow process. Use of infrared lamps above seed trays speeds drying. I also use a closed chamber made of plywood, with heat blown in from below so it flows through a stack of 2-by-2-foot screens that hold the seed.

Threshing Seed

When seeds are thoroughly dry, threshing, or loosening the seed from the surrounding plant material, is begun.

For small batches of small hard seed, place a screen over a newspaper on a flat surface and with a sanding block fitted with medium-coarse sandpaper rub out the seed.

For large batches, I use a small hammermill originally built as a leaf mulcher, made by the W. W. Grinder Co., Wichita, Kansas.

Cleaning Seed

After threshing, seed must be cleaned. The ideal is to get seed completely clean. I use five nesting screens of the following mesh sizes: $\frac{1}{32}$ inch, $\frac{1}{16}$ inch, $\frac{1}{8}$ inch, $\frac{1}{4}$ inch, and $\frac{1}{2}$ inch. For final cleaning of heavy dense seeds a simple method is to place seeds in the bottom of an 18-inch pail and carefully turn forced air from a tank-type vacuum cleaner on them, using the hose connected at the back of the tank.

By this time, it should be clear that fast, rough seed-picking means extensive threshing and cleaning later. In the long run, a quick-pick is not a time-saver.

No matter how diligent, you probably will not get your seeds 100 percent clean. But don't worry, they'll still grow.

Storing Seed

After threshing, cleaned seed must be stored for winter. Winter storage begins a series of steps that must be followed for successful germination in spring.

Prairie seeds should be stored dry, in containers that prevent moisture changes. Plastic-covered containers, such as ice cream pails, serve well. Seeds must be stored at outside temperatures during their first winter. Any unheated shed or garage, is adequate—away from rats, squirrels, and other pests, and from pets.

If you are storing seeds after the first winter, avoid heat. A refrigerator or freezer is ideal. Seeds will survive. I once obtained good germination of pasque flower seed after 4 years of refrigeration.

Treating Seed

After storage at winter temperatures, seeds have had what is called *dry stratification*. Some seeds are then ready to plant.

Prairie seeds have certain built-in germination inhibitors, protective mechanisms that prevent germination during warm fall weather. You can duplicate the natural way by planting seed in fall. But this results in uneven germination and heavy weed growth, and is not half as effective as proper stratification.

Some prairie species have hard dense seeds with a tough seedcoat that requires *scarification* (scratching of seedcoat), *moist stratification*, or both, before planting. Seeds of all members of the legume family, for example, require such treatment. (See description of species for individual requirements.) If seeds are not well scarified, they require longer moist stratification. Moist-stratified legume seeds are somewhat larger and softer than when dry.

Scarifying allows moisture to enter a seed. A good scarifier can be homemade by lining a 2-pound coffee can with sharp sandpaper. Put the seeds in the can, cover, and shake vigorously.

For moist stratification, seeds must be mixed with two or three times their volume of damp sand that has been sterilized in an oven for 1 hour at 450° F. The seeds are then placed in a moisture-proof sealed plastic bag or container, labeled with name and date, and stored in a refrigerator at 34° to 38° F. Members of the legume family must be left in the refrigerator for 10 to 15 days. Other species require from 5 to 6 weeks.

Legumes also need inoculation with nitrogen-fixing bacteria so that they can produce nitrogen and enrich the soil. (Inoculant can be purchased from The Nitrogen Co., 3101 Custer Ave., Milwaukee, WI 53209. Order by generic name, such as *Amorpha*, *Baptisia*, *Petalostemum*, etc.) The inoculant can be added to the sand and seed before or after the mixture is moist stratified.

Time stratification so that the seeds are ready to plant when you are (early June in Wisconsin).

Your seeds are now "turned on." All physiological inhibitors to germination have been removed—or should have been. If you doubt viability of any of your seeds, test them. But do so under conditions as close to natural as possible. Standard germination tests were basically designed for domestic seed and may not always work on prairie seed.

Be sure you know the history of the seeds you sow. If they have received only dry stratification, then the species requiring moist stratification will not germinate until they have overwintered in soil.

If you sow in fall, use unstratified seed collected that same year, if possible. If old seed which has been stratified is used, sow in late fall (November in Wisconsin) so that no germination will occur until spring. Seedlings germinating in September and October are too small to stand the stress of winter.

Examining Performance

Eventually, most seeds germinate. Some, prairie larkspur for instance, are temperamental and germinate whenever they please. This kind of behavior is not unusual for wild seed. Wild seed differs from domestic: domestic seed over the years has undergone a process of artificial selection; wild seed has undergone a process of natural selection.

Alfalfa seed, for example, germinates easily and uniformly. Plant breeders have eliminated the unpredictable. If you sow a hundred alfalfa seeds, almost all will germinate within a few days. If you sow a hundred leadplant seeds, only about 80 percent will germinate within a few days even though all were properly treated. The remainder may take 2 weeks, a month, 2 months, a year, even 2 years. This sporadic germination ensures survival. Should disaster strike the first seeds to germinate, the remainder will propagate the species. It is a survival method by which prairie plants over thousands of years have adapted to adversity. But "survival" does cause a prairie gardener some anxious moments.

4

Raising Your Own Plants

Sowing seed is not the only way to launch a prairie landscape project. You may buy young plants from a nursery (see source list) and transplant them where you see fit. This is a quick, efficient method, albeit more expensive than sowing seed. (Generally, it is not a good idea to collect your own plants from the wild. Many mature prairie plants have deep roots and are almost impossible to move. More important, the danger of destroying an ancient natural area is too great.)

You can also raise your own plants from seed, using various techniques, depending on your needs and circumstances.

Greenhouses

At one time I considered a greenhouse a necessity for raising my own plants. So in 1974 I built a 12-by-16-foot greenhouse for about $2,000, not counting my own labor. The following spring between early April and early May I spent some $60 to heat it, plus the cost of electricity for a cooling fan. Wisconsin winters being what they are, I did not attempt to use it year round.

However, even with limited use, problems began cropping up. Disease was one of them. Because of the crowded and humid conditions, damping off (fungal disease) occurred and chemicals had to be used to control it. Unfortunately, once an artificial factor is introduced into plant production, it may create additional problems.

One spring a planting of poppy mallow started in the greenhouse became infected with rust. Treatment did not help. In desperation, I transplanted 700 of the seedlings outdoors; I left one flat with one last treatment in the greenhouse for experimental purposes. In 10 days the young plants outdoors had recovered; the greenhouse plants were dead. What's more, poppy mallow seeded directly outdoors on June 1 compared favorably with that started in the greenhouse on April 15.

But a greenhouse does have its uses. I use mine to propagate pasque flower and prairie phlox, both of which grow slowly in their first few months. I also use the greenhouse for plants I am propagating for the first time as well as for those for which I have very little seed. For instance, I started my first psoralea seeds in the greenhouse so I could watch them closely. Now I sow them and almost everything else outdoors. I suggest you do the same.

If you decide a greenhouse is useful, construction should incorporate the latest solar technology for both heating and cooling.

Flats

When I do plant seed in the greenhouse I use flats made of redwood 10 by 16 by 3½ inches deep with bottoms of ¼-inch Masonite board into which I drill four or five ¼-inch holes. This size handles easily and the covers (10-by 16-inch glass) are available precut at a hardware store.

Because the soil in flats should be sterile, I buy prepared sterile soil that contains some fertility. It is a mixture of sand and peat. I tried sterilizing my own soil, baking it at 450° F for 1 hour. But buying it prepared saves time, trouble, and energy. This soil can also be used as a rooting medium for cuttings.

I fill the flats with soil ½ inch from the top and scatter the seeds on the surface, aiming for 100 seedlings per flat. Next, I cover the seed with fine sand from a large jar with a shaker top, and water the soil-sand. The easiest way to water is to put the flat into a large container; this allows the water to soak through the bottom holes and cracks. When the soil surface has darkened, the soil is saturated. I then set the flat on a table, cover it with a glass over which I place a folded newspaper, and wait for the seeds to germinate. The soil in the flat needs no further watering until after germination.

Prairie seeds germinate best at daytime temperatures of 70° to 80° F and night temperatures of 45° to 60° F. This diurnal variation, similar to early June weather in Wisconsin, is important. Germination is often poor in the hot days and nights of July and August.

After the seeds germinate in 10 to 20 days, I remove the glass cover and sprinkle them lightly with water as often as needed. I also keep a close watch. If the seedlings have a healthy dark green color, it means all is well, and I do nothing. If they look pale and sickly, I give them a little liquid fertilizer.

Peat pots can be substituted for flats with satisfactory results. They take more space than flats, but allow easy transplanting with little loss of plants. However, they are expensive.

I keep seedlings in the flats until they are big and sturdy enough to handle and transplant easily, usually from 2 to 3 months.

Shade Sheds

Next to the greenhouse I have a shade shed made of redwood, with corner posts set in concrete. Covering the top and sides is snow fence especially built to keep out 57 percent of the sunlight. Under the shed is a well and a pump.

I use the shed to provide seedlings shelter from sun and wind and for hardening them off after removal from the greenhouse. Flats can be started and maintained there. Because the shed has a water supply and protection, I also use it in summer for cuttings if the greenhouse gets too hot.

A shade shed or some facsimile makes raising your own transplants easier, but it is not essential.

Sowing Seed for Transplants

Although I sow most seeds outdoors during the first week of June, I sow Indiangrass, switchgrass, and big and little bluestem from June 25 to July 5 so that the roots are not too large to transplant, and prairie-dock seed, compassplant, and other *Silphium* species about August 5.

The larger the seed, the deeper it goes into the soil. Small seeds, such as leadplant and blackeyed susan, should be sown about ¼ inch deep; *Baptisia* species, about ½ inch; and lupine, ¾ inch. There is no need to measure. Prairie seeds adjust well to rough estimates. If I'm sowing moist-stratified seed, I add dry sand to thin out the mixture.

I space rows from 10 to 20 inches apart, wide enough so that two trips with a cultivator will cover the space. Rows are sown thickly. What I want are transplants. If I end up with 20 to 30 seedlings per foot, so much the better. The row itself can be from one seedling wide to a number of seedlings wide (3 to 4 inches). The wider row is fine for heavy production, particulaly with grasses and *Liatris* species. I use wooden stakes with cord for marking rows—old-fashioned perhaps, but simple, adjustable, and efficient.

After sowing and covering the seed, I firm and water the soil and do not allow it to dry until the plants are established. A light mulch over the rows helps to retain moisture. Most prairie seed that have been properly handled will germinate in 10 days; some will be visible in 4 or 5 days. If they take longer, don't give up.

If you hold seedlings over winter for transplanting in spring, do not allow them to dry out. Doing so can result in severe winterkill, especially of the shallow-rooted species, such as violets, alumroot, and pasque flower. If the soil is dry to a depth of 6 to 7 inches, irrigate it until it is moist. Irrigation in cool weather does not require much water because evaporation and transpiration is slight.

Mulching

Mulching on each side of the rows of young plants is helpful in retaining moisture. I use sawdust, shredded white pine needles, and sometimes grass clippings or other shredded matter.

Mulch improves the water-holding capacity of sandy soils and makes heavy soils more workable. Mulch can be applied fresh, as composted material, or as both. Mulch applied fresh may reduce available nitrogen during decomposition. If this occurs, apply liquid fertilizer.

Fertilizing

Although prairie plants can grow on soils of low fertility and at pH's less than 7, they respond well to fertilization. Sometimes they respond too well. I fertilize when seedlings are firmly established and then only if they do not appear healthy or are growing too slowly. I use liquid 20-20-20 fertilizer that I apply with a sprinkling can directly on the seedlings and the surrounding soil. Mulch also adds fertility, but it is slower-acting and longer-lasting than fertilizer and not as easy to control.

Frost Heaving

I have observed spring frost heaving of 1-year-old leadplant, purple prairie clover, white prairie clover, and butterfly weed. The plants are lifted just enough to expose terminal buds, which freeze. Butterfly weed will develop new buds, but the freezing is fatal to leadplant and prairie clovers.

Frost heaving can be prevented by lightly applying hay, sawdust, or other mulch in fall or very early spring. (On permanent sites, the plants are protected by an accumulation of dead plant material, so frost heaving does not often occur.)

Holding Transplants

If transplanting must be delayed, seedlings should either be refrigerated or placed in a heeling bed.

Refrigeration is a technique long used by nurseries to store plants prior to transplanting. It does them no harm. In 1976, for instance, I dug 100 butterfly weed seedlings on May 7, packed them in damp burlap, tucked them inside a plastic bag, and put them in a refrigerator at just above 32° F. The butterfly weed seedlings were removed from the refrigerator on July 14 and transplanted. Eighty-nine survived. Some species can be stored even longer. I have kept prairie rose and bottle gentian over winter with no ill effects.

The heeling bed is another nursery technique for short-term or overwinter storage. A V-shaped trench with one side slanted and the other perpendicular is dug about a foot deep. Transplants are placed on the slanting side, spread evenly, and covered with soil; only small portions of the stems are exposed. The transplants then are watered and mulched. Usually, the procedure works well, but there are exceptions. Butterfly weed, for example, often becomes moldy in a heeling bed, and should be refrigerated.

Dividing Plants

After 2 years or more, a substantial number of prairie plants, at least 50 percent of the common ones, can be increased by dividing them. Most can be divided by hand. I leave short stems for handles when cutting off tops of plants. I then grasp the handle and pull down and out. Each division should have a bud and a root. This type of division is used for clump-forming species, such as goldenrod and asters. A sharp knife is helpful with others, such as shootingstar, gentian, alumroot, and sometimes violets. Because divisions are larger and stronger than seedlings, they make ideal transplanting stock. However, prairie plants have extensive root systems that toughen as they grow older. Some species become impossible to divide after 3 or 4 years.

Producing Seed

Producing seed is a natural follow-up to producing your own transplants. It offers many advantages compared to collecting seed in the wild and is considerably less expensive than buying seed. Moisture and fertility can be controlled; this results in higher germination than in the wild. Then, of course, producing your own seed saves time. No need to prowl highways and byways.

Pollination is not a problem. Prairie plants are highly attractive to bees, butterflies, and other pollinating insects. When plants of one species are placed in rows for seed production, concentrations of these insects are spectacular. The first occurs in late May when lupine blooms. The highest is in mid and late summer when the *Liatris* species and butterfly weed are in flower. In late summer and early fall asters and goldenrod are the insects' targets.

Prairie plants increase their ability to produce seed as they grow older. I establish permanent patches of the common grasses, plus those whose seeds are not easy to collect in the wild. My patch of little bluestem is large enough for me to use a combine on it, so I leave an extra 20 feet around the perimeter for easy operation.

Grasses planted in rows 20 inches apart are satisfactory seed producers. I give the patches spring applications of balanced fertilizer, such as 10-10-10, at the rate of 100 pounds per acre, as well as occasionally irrigating them during dry periods. I weed the patches three or four times a season and pay particular attention to eliminating tall domestic weeds that would contaminate grass seed.

Forbs, too, I line out in permanent rows for seed production. They require only occasional irrigation and soil of modest fertility.

Pests

Pests are a greater problem if you are raising transplants and plants for seed production than they are in a natural setting because of the high concentrations of plants of the same species. The mammalian pests that continually visit us are deer, moles, and rabbits.

Deer do damage by trampling all plants. They also browse heavily on New Jersey tea and eat pasque flower buds. In an effort to keep deer out at night, I tie our English setter to a doghouse on the south edge of the area. This arrangement is only partially effective. I have also tried lion scent; it works until the deer get used to the smell—3 or 4 days. Fencing is the only effective way of keeping out deer, but it is expensive and bothersome.

Rabbits, in my experience, do real damage only to white prairie clover. Brer Rabbit will take this plant down to ground level, but will not touch purple prairie clover. I protect the white clover with chicken wire 18 inches high. Our cat also helps control rabbits, along with mice. We do sacrifice a few birds, but well-fed cats like ours are not especially enthusiastic hunters of elusive prey.

Moles are a serious threat in the early growing season. They love to tunnel under the loosened soil of transplants: this leaves roots dangling in the tunnels. Moles can be controlled both by traps and by commercial poisons. However, moles are predators of cutworms and white grubs, so I limit control (use traps) to the specific area where they are doing damage.

Toads are able predators of garden insects. I encourage them by placing water-filled pans and three-sided shelters on the north side of rows of perennials.

Insects that have caused me brief problems include cutworms, white grubs, red spider, and a small furry caterpillar that defoliates, preferring leaves of yellow coneflower and purple coneflower. My insect control program is based on daily inspections. This gives me a chance to take immediate action and prevent a problem from getting out of hand. Actually, insects do a great deal more good than harm by handling the pollination necessary for a good seed crop. They also add interest. Under no circumstnaces do I recommend a spraying program with nonbiodegradable chemical sprays. To control small outbreaks, I use biodegradable insecticides such as Rotenone or Pyrethrum. Cutworms and white grubs can be controlled by fall and spring cultivation.

Insects and disease problems increase if plants are not growing well. Check moisture and fertility. Severe problems can be discussed with plant pathologists at the state Department of Agriculture.

5

Planting and Maintaining a Prairie Site

Grass to Forb Ratio

How many different species does it take to make a natural-looking prairie planting? In a study of 65 prairie relics in Wisconsin, of 237 species, only 19 occurred in 50 percent or more of the stands.

Some prairie gardeners, however, prefer a greater variety of species. I am one of them. Combining at least 5 to 7 species of grasses and 15 to 20 species of forbs appeals to me. Acceptable grass to forb ratios lie between 60 to 40 and 90 to 10. Forbs make their best showing amidst grasses. Some forbs need grasses for support. The 60 to 40 ratio apparently is the most common on small areas. I recommend a ratio between 70 to 30 and 80 to 20. Over a period of years, you can expect a change in this ratio in favor of grasses.

In selecting forbs, I lean heavily on members of the Daisy family and on the legumes. They are sturdy and dependable. The legumes also have a nitrogen-fixing, soil-improving capability. (See the descriptions of individual species for height, color, and flowering periods.)

Seeding Rates

It is very difficult to make specific recommendations for the amount of seed needed to establish a prairie planting. Seeds vary greatly in quality from year to year, particularly if collected in the wild. Some batches of seed are clean; others are not. Every proposed site differs. Some sites have erosion problems; others do not. Weather patterns change. Some growing seasons are dry; others are not. All of these variables affect germination and survival.

For many years, in Nebraska and neighboring states, prairie grasses have been planted for livestock feed. Basic agricultural methods, including mechanical seeding and harvesting, have been developed for the major grass species. Their seeding rates are based on the Pure Live Seed (PLS) concept. If seed is 50 percent viable, 16 pounds per acre would be planted to obtain a coverage of 8 pounds per acre. (The number of seeds per pound of 17 selected forbs and 7 grasses is given in the list on page 207.)

Similar efforts are being used in prairie establishment. Most small prairie stands, however, are still planted by hand, and seeding rates vary widely.

Curiously, after several years the prairies themselves do not always reflect this variation. It appears to me that prairie plants make their own adjustments.

This adjustment also takes place among members of the same species. In 1974, for example, I planted a stand of little bluestem for seed production on a site 35 by 180 feet. The seed was sown in rows 20 inches apart, spread evenly, and covered. In the first 2 years the rows appeared solid. But after 4 years they formed clumps 8 to 9 inches in diameter at the base and stood 3 to 5 inches apart. So they remain.

Closely crowded forbs in their second and third years also seem to thin themselves by developing fewer complete dominants.

Recommended seeding rates for grasses vary. Rates for little bluestem, for example, vary from .75 pounds per acre to 15 pounds per acre. If techniques were available to get maximum results from little bluestem seed, 1 pound would be more than adequate to cover 1 acre. Since such techniques presently are not available, I recommend 5 pounds per acre. My other recommendations include the following:

Grass	Pounds per acre
Big bluestem	4.0
Sideoats grama	4.0
Junegrass	0.5
Switchgrass	1.0
Indiangrass	1.0
Prairie dropseed	1.0
Needlegrass	2.0

On light soils the rates can be reduced by one-third. These recommendations are made on the basis of seeds being sown separately, not in mixes.

Sowing Seed on Small Areas

Prairie seeds sown on small areas (up to 2500 square feet) can be sprinkled in the same way you would seed a small patch of lawn. Follow your design plan and put the seeds, by species, where you want them.

You can also spot-seed. Take a pinch of seed, cover ¼ to ½ inch deep, and firm the soil over the seeds. Space grasses 12 to 15 inches apart, and place forbs between the grasses according to your plan.

Or you can both sprinkle and spot-seed. For example, you might begin with sprinkling little bluestem, an all-purpose warm-season grass, then go over the prepared site two or more times to get even coverage. Next, on a dry or a mesic site, you might spot-seed rough blazingstar, dwarf blazingstar, leadplant, and purple prairie clover.

Do not mix seeds. Some species are aggressive and will take over where sown. (See descriptions of individual species.) Isolate these species. Place them with competitive companion plants, always with a design plan in mind. Mixing seeds with light-colored sand or fine vermiculite helps show what has been covered and helps extend small amounts of seed. Try for a coverage of 4 to 5 seeds per square foot. After sowing, cover seeds by raking and rolling to firm the soil.

Make sure at least two plantings of each species are labeled. Not only does labeling make identification possible as plants emerge, but neglecting to label may mean loss of precious plants to over-zealous weeders. Labels are also a great help in comparing the respective merits of individual species. And labels help in associating species names and characteristics until they become familiar. There are many kinds of labels on the market. Take your pick. Or make your own. But do label.

During the first year it may be necessary to thin forb seedlings, but most will adjust to crowding. Because prairie grass seedlings develop as a single clump, even if more than one plant is present, thinning is not necessary.

Irrigation of a seed-sown area is desirable for a few weeks because some of the seeds may have been moist stratified and should not be allowed to dry out. When seedlings have their first true leaves, irrigation can be reduced or discontinued.

Sowing Seed on Large Areas

Hand-broadcasting makes a handsome prairie landscape because the seeding can be patterned in an aesthetically pleasing manner. However, hand-broadcasting is practical up to about 2 acres. Any larger area has to be seeded mechanically, unless you have a crew willing to do hand work.

The procedure for broadcasting seed by hand remains the same as that used by farmers to plant grain a hundred years ago. With seed bag over his shoulder, the sower walked his field, throwing seeds ahead of him with a half-circle motion of his whole arm. For the most even coverage, I suggest broadcasting prairie seed in the early morning when winds are down. Some planters like a slight breeze so that the seeds can drift naturally.

A hand-operated whirlwind seeder is very useful in seeding dense seeds, but not fluffy ones. It is excellent for sowing legumes, for flowering spurge, bergamot, dotted mint, yellow coneflower, and spiderwort, and if seed is fairly clean, for switchgrass and prairie dropseed.

I have had no experience with mechanical seed-planters for prairies, but I know they produce more even coverage and make more economical use of seed. Use of mechanical planters, however, does result in rigid patterns. To achieve a more natural look, you might crisscross the rows and vary the design by spot-seeding by hand. After hand-seeding, the soil must be lightly dragged and firmed with a cultipacker.

Most large areas cannot be irrigated easily. For best results, seeding should be timed for fast germination and early growth before the hot dry part of summer begins. (In Wisconsin, the prime period to seed a large area would be late May to the first week in June—about 2 weeks after corn planting. With perennial weed control, mid-May seeding has advantages.) Earlier seeding takes advantage of rainfall, but too-cool weather slows germination.

A cover, or nurse, crop gives early shade to emerging prairie plants, helps keep down weeds, and helps control erosion from wind and rain. Oats work well as a nurse crop. Oats are inexpensive, available, and ready to cut when the prairie plants are established. Sow oats at one-half normal rate, about 1½ bushels per acre, either broadcast or drilled prior to the prairie plant seeding. Wild rye, a natural prairie plant, is also a satisfactory cover crop; sow it at about 2½ pounds per acre. Wild rye, however, will persist for many years and, to me, is not attractive. If a site has been inhabited for any length of time, it probably contains thousands of seeds of annual weeds that germinate and produce seed in 1 year. These annual weeds can also serve as a nurse crop that disappears when the prairie plants take over.

Using Transplants

Transplants are practical in small areas (2500 square feet or less). Although they are more expensive, as well as more work than seeds, in most cases you will have bloom the first year. Weeds, however, must be controlled by hand.

Transplanting should be done when a plant is dormant, in fall or spring. Transplanting in fall (October or November in Wisconsin) usually is more successful because a plant is fully dormant and will not be ready to grow until exposed to winter cold and spring warmth. Early spring (April in Wisconsin) is better than late spring when plants have begun growing.

If you dig your own transplants, be sure to get as much of the root system as you can. (I use a short-handled 16-inch tile-laying shovel with a rounded point.) Shake transplants free of soil, and immediately place them inside a fold of dampened burlap. Then take them into the shade to sort, divide, and root-prune.

I prune all broken roots and all excessively long roots. After one season of growth, pruned roots show a proliferation of new roots from the point of cutting. Root pruning also makes transplanting easier.

In transplanting, make sure the soil has been tilled deep enough so that digging is easy. Keep all plants moist and protected from sun. A gray windless day is ideal for transplanting.

Dig individual holes deep enough so the roots of the plants will not be curled up and so the terminal buds will be covered with about an inch of soil. Proceed slowly. Give your fingers time to get the feel of what you are doing. Pack the soil as you fill the hole, firming it around the roots to work out the air pockets. With your plan in mind, measure or estimate the spacing as you go. After completing a small section, tamp the soil and water the transplanted area. After a day's work, water, and water again, in the evening. (Be sure to label at least two plants of each species for later identification.)

Signs of growth should appear within 10 days to 2 weeks, depending on species and weather conditions. Then the transplants should do well, unless the weather becomes very hot and dry. If it does, continue watering throughout the summer.

If the young plants yellow or show a lack of vigor, apply a liquid fertilizer. Repeat this only if you think it necessary. But guard against over-fertilizing. The loss of good seedlings is usually due to wrong transplanting procedures, lack of care, or to both.

Prairie Remnants

You may be lucky enough to have an area with a limited number of prairie species or with widely scattered prairie plants. These are prairie remnants, sometimes called old field successions; they are common in sand country. This type of area, originally sand prairie, probably was cropped once or twice, then abandoned because of low productivity. Some prairie plants survived because dormant seed or root parts remained in the soil. The species most commonly found in these areas are strong seeders and persistent growers. In Wisconsin sand country, these plants usually include big bluestem, little bluestem, bush clover, dotted mint, pussytoes, flowering spurge, spiderwort, and Junegrass, with grass cover often dominated by three-awn grass (*Aristida* sp.). Often more species are present, with cool-season grasses and other weeds absent. Such areas were once viewed with consternation. Almost a prairie, but not quite. What to do?

Prairie remnant sites can be made more attractive by the introduction of more species. The area should be disked or rototilled very lightly, just enough to disturb the open soil, but not enough to dig up existing prairie plants. Then the field can be seeded (by hand or with a special drill) with a general cover of little bluestem, and spot-seeded with other grasses and forbs. After seeding, the area must be dragged lightly to cover the seed. Fall or early spring is the best time to begin to convert your site. After a year or so you should be able to see what you have, what you need, and what you want. Desired species can be added by spot-seeding or by transplanting. (Years ago farmers added legumes to winter grain stands by seeding in very early spring either by hand or with a whirlwind seeder. The freezing and thawing of the ground, along with spring rains, helped to cover the seed. The same process could be used with small dense prairie seeds.)

29

Many of these remnant sites are so infertile that they will not support a large number of plants per acre, therefore seeding should be light. Even a hardy plant such as rough blazingstar (*Liatris aspera*) has trouble the first year or two after being transplanted into these areas. This may be one of the few times that fertilizer, applied lightly, would help. In theory, these areas should gradually be fertilized by plant decomposition. Legumes, especially lupine, have this proclivity.

On fertile remnant sites, planting is not easy because of the increased possibility of heavy infestation of domestic cool-season grasses or other weeds mixed with the prairie plants.

Weed Control

Whatever the size or the type of prairie planting, during the first summer, weed control is the biggest job. On large areas, cutting is done with farm machinery. On small areas, weeding is a hand job done with hand tools, supplemented with mowing.

Mowing may be done with a rotary mower set 5 to 8 inches or high enough so that it will not injure the prairie species. Weeds or cover crops should be mowed before they become too tall or dense; this is about 30 days after planting. Mow two or three more times if necessary. On small areas where mowing is impossible, a scythe or a hand clipper will do the job, but the clippings must be removed.

If a site has been properly prepared for planting, weeds should be mainly annuals from seed in the ground. Mowing shreds the tops, removes the shade, and destroys the weed seed crop.

If you have perennial weeds, as you might on a prairie remnant, they may be removed by hand. However, the most effective method is the very careful application of a tested herbicide.

If your small prairie site is bordered by cool-season domestic grasses, they will invade if they can. You can control them by burying 8-inch sheet aluminum vertically just below the soil surface.

On large areas, a disked or plowed strip 6 to 10 feet wide around the area will control invaders and serve as a firebreak as well.

Other than adding needed prairie species, do *not* disturb the soil. Digging, cultivating, or both will produce a whole new crop of annual weeds.

Maintenance

Success of seedling growth depends largely on the ability of seedlings to develop efficient root systems. Little bluestem, for example, under favorable conditions has a primary root 2 to 2½ inches underground before a shoot appears above ground. Not every prairie plant shows up well the first year. Some have difficulty establishing themselves. Some may not germinate until conditions are suitable. Germination may take a second year or more. But stand by, be patient. Keep track of what you have, keep watering when and where possible, and protect young plants from trampling feet. Incidentally, young prairie grasses change color dramatically after the first killing frost and are easy to spot even in a mixture of weeds. This should add a note of encouragement the first fall.

By the second year, the site will show signs of looking and acting like a prairie. The grasses will bloom and bear seed. Many of the colorful forbs will blossom. In the second year inspect each species regularly to see if you have the right plant in the right place. This is a time to add what you think you need.

Annual domestic weeds may continue to compete with the prairie species during the second year. To control them, mow in late June; leaving a stubble of 5 to 8 inches as you did the first year. This will cut back the early-growing annual weeds, but will not affect the slower-growing prairie plants.

Often, prairie stands may be invaded by trees or shurbs. In my area, for instance, invaders include jack pine, Hill's oak, and staghorn sumac. When removing jack pine, I've found it necessary to remove the whole tree from the site. Otherwise the cones will open over a period of years and young jack pine will sprout from seed all over the place. I control oak and sumac by selective use of herbicides.

During the third year, new plants can be added, but the prairie should then be closing in and crowding out the competition.

After the third year, or the fourth, burning can be considered on large sites where feasible. Before burning, you will have to check for needed permits and get advice from fire control personnel. You will need to redisk the firebreak as well as have help and fire-fighting equipment on hand. (A snow shovel serves as a good fire beater.) Be sure to choose a late afternoon when the wind is calm and the temperature cool.

Burning usually is done in early spring (April 5 to 20 in Wisconsin) every 3 or 4 years, depending on conditions. On light soils it may be less often. Burning only half the prairie in 1 year protects wildlife.

In spring, a burned prairie heats up quickly, and growth is stimulated. Large quantities of organic matter are converted to plant nutrients that make a prairie stand brighter, cleaner, and greener than it would be without them. Burning also discourages cool-season domestic grasses and woody invaders, thus tipping the balance in favor of the prairie species.

On a small site if burning is inadvisable, you can remove accumulated waste by cutting and raking in early spring.

By the fourth year most of a prairie gardener's work is finished. The prairie plants should be able to fend for themselves, in an incredibly persistent manner. So, except for an occasional clean-up, there is little to do except enjoy your prairie landscape.

Allium cernuum

Amorpha canescens

Anemone patens

Anemone cylindrica

Antennaria sp.

Aquilegia canadensis

Asclepias amplexicaulis

Asclepias incarnata

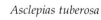

Asclepias tuberosa

Aster ericoides

Aster novae-angliae

Aster sericeus

Astragalus canadensis

Baptisia leucantha

Baptisia leucophaea

Callirhoe triangulata

Ceanothus americanus

Coreopsis palmata   *Delphinium virescens*   *Dodecatheon meadia*

Echinacea pallida (top left)

Echinacea purpurea (top right)

Euphorbia corollata (center)

Eryngium yuccifolium (lower left)

Filipendula rubra (lower right)

Gentiana andrewsii

Geum triflorum

Helianthus occidentalis

Heuchera richardsonii

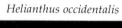

Hudsonia tomentosa

Iris shrevei

Lespedeza capitata

Liatris aspera

40

Liatris cylindracea (left)

Liatris pycnostachya (right)

Lilium superbum (left)

Lithospermum croceum (rig

Lupinus perennis (left)

Monarda fistulosa (right)

Monarda punctata

Oenothera biennis

Petalostemum candidum   *Petalostemum purpureum*

Phlox pilosa

Psoralea esculenta

Ranunculus rhomboideus

Ratibida pinnata

Rosa sp.

Rudbeckia hirta

Silphium laciniatum (left)

Silphium perfoliatum (right)

Silphium terebinthinaceum

Sisyrinchium campestre

Solidago nemoralis

Solidago rigida

Solidago speciosa

Tephrosia virginiana

Vernonia fasciculata

45

Tradescantia ohiensis

Veronicastrum virginicum

Viola pedata

Viola pedata (bi-color)

Andropogon gerardi

Andropogon scoparius

Bouteloua curtipendula

Koeleria cristata

Panicum virgatum

Sorghastrum nutans

Sporobolus heterolepis

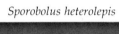

47

Stipa spartea

Carex pensylvanica
(surrounding clump
of *Panicum virgatum*)

Landscape,
the Wade home

The Prairie
Nursery
in July

A Guide
to the
Species

Names

Common, as well as scientific, names are given for each plant discussed in this section. Most species have a number of common names. Often the same common name is applied to several different species in various regions or even in the same region. Spelling, too, is a matter of preference, usage, and readability.

Height, Color, Flowering Time, Seed Collection Date

Prairie plants are variable. Height, color, flowering time, and seed collection date of the same species may differ from one season to the next and from one area to another. Therefore, information given under these headings is necessarily only approximate.

Seed Treatment, Propagation

Seed treatment and propagation procedures are methods, developed over several years at Prairie Nursery, which have proved successful. However, stratification requirements may vary for seeds of the same species collected in different geographic areas. If certain seeds do not germinate after dry stratification, they may do so after moist stratification.

Companion Plants

Companion plants are those plants which prefer the same environment and grow together in harmony. Only a few companion plants for each species are mentioned. A complete list would be nearly endless. In preparing the list, I have drawn on *Plants of the Chicago Region* by Floyd Swink (Suggested Reading), in addition to my own observations in Wisconsin. Since these associations vary from one area to another, this information should be supplemented by study of prairie plant associates in your own locality.

Comment

All prairie plants have special qualities and fascinating histories. Some even seem destined to be significant in man's struggle for survival. Such facts are noted under "Comment."

Forbs
and Shrubs

Prairie forbs and shrubs are flowering plants which generally are perennial. Each has a pair of opposite cotyledons (first leaves), stems which thicken with age, and flower parts occurring mostly in fours and fives. The shrubs described here (*Amorpha canescens*, *Ceanothus americanus*, and *Rosa* sp.) can be recognized by their woody stems, which branch at or near the ground. The higher orders of both forbs and shrubs are insect-pollinated, the lower orders wind-pollinated.

$\times$ 1   Color photograph, p. 33

Allium cernuum

COMMON NAMES: Nodding Pink Onion; Ladys-leek; Wild Onion
KIND OF PRAIRIE: Mesic
HEIGHT: 1 to 2 feet
COLOR OF FLOWER: Pale pink to white
FLOWERING TIME: July to August: from bulbs, the first year; from seed, the second year
SEED COLLECTION DATE: September to October
SEED TREATMENT: Moist stratification results in more uniform germination.
PROPAGATION: Easily propagated from seed and by separating offset bulbs from parent plant. To produce transplants, sow stratified seed ¼ inch deep in spring or maintain older plants as a source of new bulbs. For permanent plantings, sow unstratified seed in fall or stratified seed in early spring, or plant small colonies of bulbs.
COMPANION PLANTS: Little Bluestem; Prairie Phlox, Spiderwort; Purple Prairie Clover
COMMENT: This lovely wild onion is especially attractive when planted in groups of a dozen or more. As blooming nears, the U-shaped stem straightens so blossom-head nods with the wind. It is as easy to grow as domestic onion, but does not do well against heavy grass competition. Nor does it favor dry upland sand.

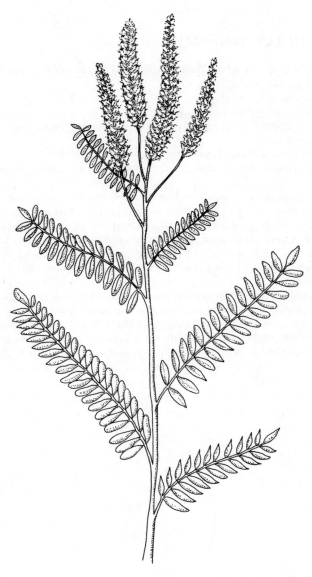

× ½   Color photograph, p. 33

Amorpha canescens (A legume)

COMMON NAMES: Leadplant; Shoestring; Wild Tea
KIND OF PRAIRIE: Dry; Mesic
HEIGHT: 18 inches to 3 feet
COLOR OF FLOWER: Dense lavender florets. (Silvery green leaves.)
FLOWERING TIME: Mid-June to mid-July: from seed, the fourth to fifth year
SEED COLLECTION DATE: Late August to October
SEED TREATMENT: Scarification, inoculation, moist stratification for 10 days. Seeds can also be soaked in water at 180° F and allowed to cool. Soaking treatment is faster, but does not give as high or as uniform germination.
PROPAGATION: Best propagated from seed. To produce transplants, seed should be sown thickly ¼ inch deep in the spring (early June in Wisconsin). For permanent plantings, 6- to 8-inch transplants work well. Transplant 1-year-old roots with buds at least 2 inches deep. Can also sow unstratified seed in the fall or stratified seed in spring.
COMPANION PLANTS: Almost all other dry prairie species, especially Butterfly Weed; Purple Prairie Clover; Sideoats; Pasque Flower
COMMENT: This superior, classical, dry prairie plant has attractive blossoms. Bushy foliage blends with all species. It is a strong survivor, with a very deep single or branching taproot. Seed closely resembles that of alfalfa, but is smaller. Sprouts can be grown in flats and eaten like alfalfa sprouts.

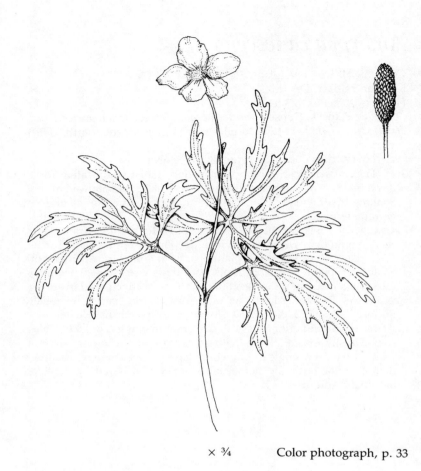

$\times$ ¾   Color photograph, p. 33

Anemone cylindrica

COMMON NAMES: Thimbleweed; Candle Anemone
KIND OF PRAIRIE: Dry; Mesic
HEIGHT: 12 to 24 inches
COLOR OF FLOWER: Greenish white
FLOWERING TIME: Mid-June to mid-July: from transplants, the first year; from seed, the second year
SEED COLLECTION DATE: Mid-August to October
SEED TREATMENT: Dry stratification
PROPAGATION: Easily propagated from seed; older plants can be divided. Transplants can be produced in one growing season from cottony seed sown ¼ inch deep in early spring. For permanent plantings, use transplants in fall or early spring, or sow seed in fall or early spring.
COMPANION PLANTS: Leadplant; Silky Aster; Sideoats; Flowering Spurge
COMMENT: This interesting, hardy member of the Buttercup family has petal-like sepals, long thin stalks, and slender, thimblelike seedheads. The seedhead bursts into tiny cascades of white cottony material when ripe. If picked early enough, the seedheads dry well and are attractive additions to winter bouquets. Tea from roots of this plant is said to be helpful for dizzy spells.

$\times$ ¾ Color photograph, p. 33

Anemone patens

COMMON NAMES: Pasque Flower; Windflower; Easter Flower; Wild Crocus

KIND OF PRAIRIE: Dry; Mesic

HEIGHT: 3 to 6 inches

COLOR OF FLOWER: Pale lavender with yellow-orange center disk

FLOWERING TIME: April: from seed, after 2 years of growth

SEED COLLECTION DATE: May to early June

SEED TREATMENT: Fresh or dry stratification

PROPAGATION: Best propagated from seed. To produce transplants, seed should be placed in flats and lightly covered with sand, hoping for 75 to 100 plants per 10-by 16-inch flat. Flats must be kept moist and protected with glass and newspaper. Seedlings appear within 10 days to 2 weeks. They should be kept in flats for about 12 weeks, at which time they are about 3 or 4 inches high and ready for transplanting to a holding bed. They should be kept in the holding bed until fall of the same year or early spring of the following year before being moved to a permanent site. For permanent plantings, use transplants in fall or early spring. If transplanted in fall, young plants should have a light application of liquid fertilizer because they are forming new buds for early spring growth. Mulching helps, as does mixing 1 teaspoon of lime per plant with the soil.

COMPANION PLANTS: Leadplant; Prairie Smoke; Prairie Dropseed; Dwarf Blazingstar

COMMENT: The large, delicate flower of this plant appears on a short stem before any leaf growth, sometimes immediately after a spring snowstorm in Wisconsin. This plant prefers dry sandy slopes with good drainage and will not tolerate water-logged soil. It does not like heavy grass competition or other heavy shade-producing vegetation, but it does like open oak shade. Seed production is greatly improved if the plant is protected from high winds. Best growth comes in cool weather of spring and fall. It is an ideal plant in dry rock gardens.

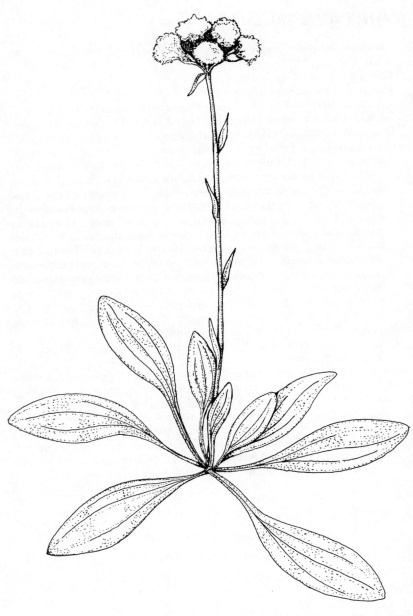

× 1   Color photograph, p. 34

Antennaria sp.

COMMON NAMES: Pussytoes; Catsfoot
KIND OF PRAIRIE: Dry; Mesic
HEIGHT: 1 to 12 inches
COLOR OF FLOWER: Creamy white
FLOWERING TIME: May
PROPAGATION: Easily divided, reproduces rapidly by rhizomes. To produce transplants, divide clumps in spring or fall, making sure each section has a bud and a root. For permanent plantings, use transplants in spring or fall.
COMPANION PLANTS: Flowering Spurge; Bush Clover
COMMENT: This highly variable, many-specied member of the Daisy family forms solid patches on dry soils, often to the exclusion of other species, and makes an interesting ground cover. Plants moved from sterile soils to soils with nutrients increase greatly in size. Clusters of small soft flowerheads resemble tiny cat's paws. At an earlier time they were stored with woolens to discourage moths, given to mothers after childbirth to stop hemorrhages, and used in shampoos to get rid of lice.

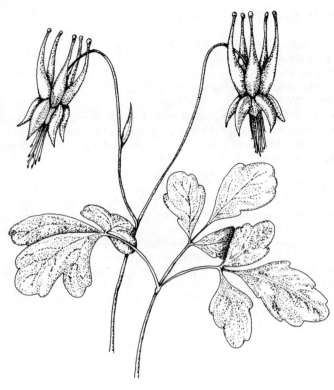

× ¾   Color photograph, p. 34

Aquilegia canadensis

COMMON NAMES: Columbine; Wild Columbine
KIND OF PRAIRIE: Dry; Mesic
HEIGHT: 1 to 2 feet
COLOR OF FLOWER: Orange-red and yellow
FLOWERING TIME: Variable, usually June to July: from transplants, the first year; from seed, the second year.
SEED COLLECTION DATE: Variable, July to August
SEED TREATMENT: Fresh seed, or dry stratification plus scarification
PROPAGATION: Easily propagated from seed. To produce transplants, sow seeds ¼ inch deep as soon as collected or in the following spring. Transplant size is reached in 2 to 3 months of growing weather. For permanent establishment, move young plants 5 to 8 inches high in late fall or early spring. Seed sown in fall or early spring is also satisfactory.
COMPANION PLANTS: Prairie Phlox; Alumroot; Prairie Smoke
COMMENT: Usually found in moist woods, columbine is not classified as a prairie plant. But in sand country it often grows alongside prairie phlox and alumroot. Highly satisfactory as well as beautiful, it is easy to establish in a backyard garden and guarantees visits from hummingbirds. It is a good mingler in fresh bouquets. Its leaves can be eaten as salad greens.

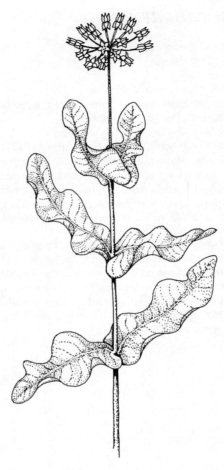

× ¼   Color photograph, p. 34

Asclepias amplexicaulis

COMMON NAMES: Blunt-leaved Milkweed; Sand Milkweed
KIND OF PRAIRIE: Dry sandy
HEIGHT: 1 to 2 feet
COLOR: Greenish purple
FLOWERING TIME: Late June to early August: from seed, the second or third year; from transplants, the first or second year
SEED COLLECTION DATE: October
SEED TREATMENT: Dry stratification
PROPAGATION: Best propagated from seed. Seed sown in early June will produce transplants by fall. Permanent plantings can be established by sowing unstratified seed in fall or stratified seed in spring, or by using year-old transplants in fall or spring.
COMPANION PLANTS: Butterfly Weed; Rough Blazingstar; Little Bluestem; Western Sunflower; Lupine
COMMENT: Not as stiffly erect or as aggressive as most milkweed, this plant is easily damaged by wind and trampling. Deer are fond of the seedheads and flowers. A brew made from the boiled root has a purging effect and was once used to treat various afflictions. The name *Asclepias* honors Aesculapius, a Greek authority on the medicinal properties of plants.

× ½   Color photograph, p. 34

Asclepias incarnata

COMMON NAMES: Red Milkweed; Swamp Milkweed; Marsh Milkweed
KIND OF PRAIRIE: Wet to Mesic
HEIGHT: 2 to 4 feet
COLOR OF FLOWER: Rose-red
FLOWERING TIME: Late June to early August: from transplants, the first
   year; from seed, the second year
SEED COLLECTION DATE: September to October
SEED TREATMENT: Dry stratification
PROPAGATION: Easily propagated from seed. Seed sown in spring (early
   June in Wisconsin) ½ inch deep will produce transplants in one sea-
   son. Plants divide well up to 4 years, then become more difficult with
   developing lateral root systems. Permanent plantings can be estab-
   lished from seed or from transplants in fall or spring.
COMPANION PLANTS: Joe-Pye Weed; Boneset; New England Aster; Big
   Bluestem; Bergamot; Culversroot; Turkscap
COMMENT: Attractive to butterflies like most milkweed, this species
   does well in garden soil and is sometimes used in perennial borders.
   The long and pointed seedpods dry nicely for winter bouquets. If
   crushed, the stem exudes a sticky milky juice used as a glue by early
   settlers and as a tea by Native Americans to treat slow lactation in
   nursing mothers.

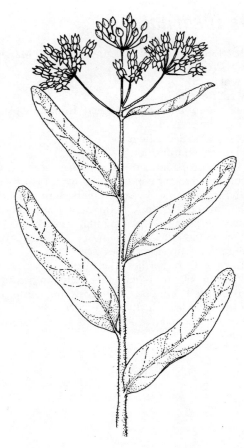

× ½   Color photograph, p. 34

Asclepias tuberosa

COMMON NAMES: Butterfly Weed; Pleurisy Root; Canada Root; Indian Posy; Orange Root; Orange Milkweed; Tuber Root; Orange Swallowwort

KIND OF PRAIRIE: Dry; Mesic

HEIGHT: 1 to 2 feet

COLOR OF FLOWER: Brilliant orange-red, sometimes yellow, sometimes white

FLOWERING TIME: Mid-June to mid-August: from seed, the second year; from transplants, the first year; flowers increase in number and size as plants grow older.

SEED COLLECTION DATE: September to October

SEED TREATMENT: Dry stratification

PROPAGATION: Best propagated from seed. To produce transplants, sow seed ½ inch deep in spring (early June in Wisconsin). There is some tendency for year-old plants to frost-heave in spring, thus exposing buds and resulting in injury; this can be controlled by use of light mulch. Transplants can also be produced from 2-inch root cuttings, treated with Rootone, planted 2 inches deep. Permanent plantings can easily be established from seed or from transplants in fall or spring.

COMPANION PLANTS: Leadplant; Little Bluestem; Junegrass; Silky Aster; Showy Goldenrod

COMMENT: This is one of the most strikingly colored prairie plants, with a rare ability for attracting butterflies. Monarchs like to lay their eggs on butterfly weed, which contains a substance poisonous to birds who will not eat the larvae. Butterfly weed is a handsome cut flower that lasts well, especially if plunged into cold water immediately after cutting. Widespread and long-lived, it is found in grasslands from New England to Arizona. Its branching taproot, an inch in diameter, is subject to a fungus that destroys the root tip and other portions of the plant. However, the damaged parts regenerate and grow as well as any, although they look rather grotesque. Boiled roots, regardless of shape, were once used to treat pleurisy and other lung troubles.

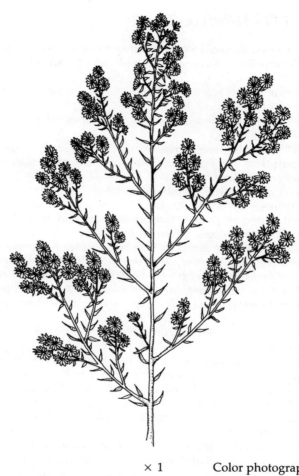

$\times$ 1   Color photograph, p. 35

Aster ericoides

COMMON NAMES: Heath Aster; Michaelmas Daisy

KIND OF PRAIRIE: Dry; Mesic

HEIGHT: 1 to 3 feet

COLOR OF FLOWER: Small white blossom, yellow disk center. (Tiny heathlike leaves.)

FLOWERING TIME: September: from transplants, the first year

SEED COLLECTION DATE: October

SEED TREATMENT: Dry stratification

PROPAGATION: Best propagated by division. Seed germination is usually poor. To produce transplants, divide mature plants; they produce numerous easily separated rhizomes. For permanent plantings, use transplants in late fall or very early spring.

COMPANION PLANTS: Coreopsis; Flowering Spurge; Purple Prairie clover; Needlegrass

COMMENT: Variable—starlike flowerheads are sometimes dense, sometimes not. I'm not sure why. The name *aster* comes from the Greek word for star. Honeybees like the flower. This aster grows on a wide variety of soils from Maine to Minnesota, and is often found along dry roadsides.

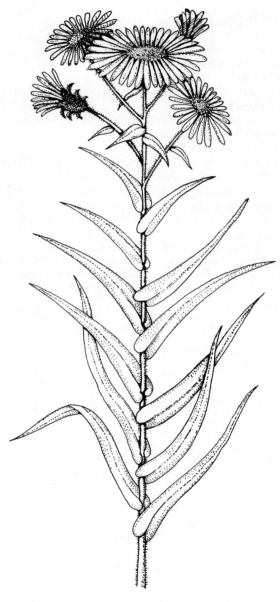

× 1   Color photograph, p. 35

Aster novae-angliae

COMMON NAME: New England Aster

KIND OF PRAIRIE: Mesic, Wet

HEIGHT: 2 to 4 feet

COLOR OF FLOWER: Deep violet, sometimes rose, with golden disk center

FLOWERING TIME: Late August to October: from transplants, the first year; from seed, the second year.

SEED COLLECTION DATE: Late October to November

SEED TREATMENT: Moist stratification improves germination.

PROPAGATION: Easily propagated either from seed or by division. Seed sown ¼ inch deep in spring (early June in Wisconsin) will produce transplants in one season. Mature plants can be easily divided. For permanent plantings, use transplants or seed sown in fall or spring.

COMPANION PLANTS: Big Bluestem; Red Milkweed; Culversroot; Rigid Goldenrod

COMMENT: This striking member of the Daisy family is extremely aggressive and needs competition. Common in roadside ditches, it also easily adjusts to dry soils. If cut back during late spring and early summer, plants will be compact and bushy rather than leggy. Butterflies and honeybees like the blossoms. A parent of many of the cultivated asters, this aster is decorative and long-lasting in either fresh or dried bouquets.

× 1   Color photograph, p. 35

Aster sericeus

COMMON NAMES: Silky Aster; Silvery Aster
KIND OF PRAIRIE: Dry to Mesic
HEIGHT: 1 to 2 feet
COLOR OF FLOWER: Rosy blue
FLOWERING TIME: Mid-September: from transplants, the first year; from seed, the second year
SEED COLLECTION DATE: Mid-October
SEED TREATMENT: Dry stratification
PROPAGATION: Best propagated by division. Seed germinates poorly. To produce transplants, divide mature plants. The plants divide more easily if located on dry sandy soil. For permanent plantings, plant divided sections in either fall or spring.
COMPANION PLANTS: Leadplant; Big Bluestem; Little Bluestem; Side-oats; Purple Prairie Clover; Prairie Dropseed
COMMENT: This welcome end-of-season bloomer has highly attractive blossoms and foliage. A hot bath containing stems and flowers of this aster is said to help arthritis sufferers.

× ½   Color photograph, p. 35

Astragalus canadensis (A legume)

COMMON NAMES: Milk-vetch; Little Rattlepod

KIND OF PRAIRIE: Dry

HEIGHT: 1 to 4 feet

COLOR OF FLOWER: Yellowish white

FLOWERING TIME: July to August: from transplants, the first year; from seed, the second year

SEED COLLECTION DATE: October

SEED TREATMENT: Scarification, inoculation, moist stratification for 10 days

PROPAGATION: Easily propagated from seed. To produce transplants, sow seed ¼ inch deep in spring (early June in Wisconsin). For permanent plantings, use 1-year-old transplants in fall or spring, or sow unstratified seed in fall or stratified seed in spring.

COMPANION PLANTS: Big Bluestem; Flowering Spurge; Bush Clover; Needlegrass

COMMENT: This is an aggressive legume with attractive foliage, a long stalk, and small flowers. It spreads rapidly and needs strong competition. Native to all parts of the United States except the Atlantic seaboard. Its boiled root was once used as a fever remedy.

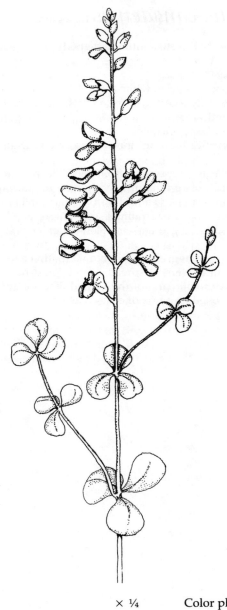

$\times \frac{1}{4}$ Color photograph, p. 35

Baptisia leucantha (A legume)

COMMON NAMES: White False Indigo; Prairie False Indigo; White Wild Indigo

KIND OF PRAIRIE: Dry; Mesic

HEIGHT: 3 to 4 feet

COLOR OF FLOWER: White

FLOWERING TIME: June: from transplants, the third or fourth year; from seed, the fourth or fifth year

SEED COLLECTION DATE: August to September

SEED TREATMENT: Scarification, inoculation, moist stratification for 10 days

PROPAGATION: Best propagated from seed first placed in refrigerator to chill seed pods, which are often infected by weevils. Seed sown ½ inch deep in spring (early June in Wisconsin) will produce transplants the first year. Large core can be divided if a bud and a root are included in each section. For permanent plantings, 1-year-old transplants are very satisfactory. Can also sow unstratified seed in fall or stratified seed in spring.

COMPANION PLANTS: Spiderwort; Indiangrass; Big Bluestem; Little Bluestem; Flowering Spurge

COMMENT: This is a sturdy, adjustable legume with a massive root system growing from a central core that can extend to 10 feet. Its floral display is best on dry sites. White blossoms can be seen for 200 yards. Most spectacular if surrounded by small species.

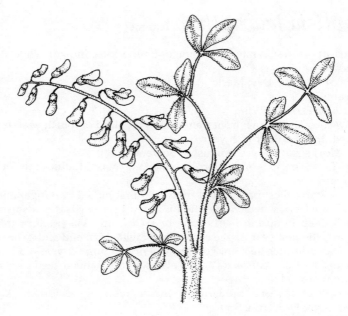

× ¼   Color photograph, p. 36

Baptisia leucophaea (A legume)

COMMON NAMES: Cream False Indigo; Black Rattlepod
KIND OF PRAIRIE: Dry; Mesic
HEIGHT: 1 to 2 feet
COLOR OF FLOWER: Creamy yellow
FLOWERING TIME: Late May to June: from transplants, the third or
fourth year; from seed, the fourth or fifth year
SEED COLLECTION: Date: August to September
SEED TREATMENT: Scarification, inoculation, moist stratification for 10
days
PROPAGATION: Best propagated from seed. To produce transplants,
place seed pods in refrigerator for several hours before removing
seed to chill seed pods, often infected by weevils. Sow seed ½ inch
deep in spring (early June in Wisconsin). For permanent plantings,
1-year-old transplants are very satisfactory. Old plants greatly increase seed production after the fifth year.
COMPANION PLANTS: Little Bluestem; Spiderwort; Leadplant; Coreopsis; Rough Blazingstar; Showy Goldenrod; Birdsfoot Violet; Bush
Clover
COMMENT: This species tends to roll and damage its foliage in the wind;
it needs support from companion plants, particularly little bluestem.
It does poorly on exposed soil. Bloom is lush, but brief. More showy
on dry sites. Foliage turns dark after a frost. Leaves yield an indigo
blue dye if steeped in water and allowed to ferment.

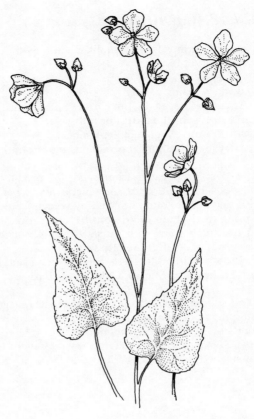

$\times$ ¼   Color photograph, p. 36

Callirhoe triangulata

COMMON NAMES: Poppy Mallow; Purple Mallow
KIND OF PRAIRIE: Dry
HEIGHT: Creeping, 1 to 2 feet
COLOR OF FLOWER: Reddish purple
FLOWERING TIME: Late June to early September: from transplants, the first year; from seed, the second year
SEED COLLECTION DATE: September to October
SEED TREATMENT: Moist stratification
PROPAGATION: Best propagated from seed. To produce transplants, sow seed ½ inch deep in spring (early June in Wisconsin). Division is difficult. For permanent plantings, 1-year-old transplants do well. Plant is somewhat rare; therefore seed is difficult to get in large quantities. If seed is available, it can be sown unstratified in fall or stratified in spring.
COMPANION PLANTS: Spiderwort; Leadplant; Little Bluestem; Big Bluestem
COMMENT: Poppy mallow is an attractive flower that blooms over a long period. Its procumbent stems turn upward at the 2-inch blooming tips. Seed produces well, likes sandy areas. The mature plant develops a deep-growing divided taproot.

× ⅓   Color photograph, p. 36

Ceanothus americanus

COMMON NAME: New Jersey Tea
KIND OF PRAIRIE: Dry; Mesic
HEIGHT: 1 to 3 feet
COLOR OF FLOWER: White
FLOWERING TIME: Late June to mid-August: from transplants, the first or second year; from seed, the third year
SEED COLLECTION DATE: September to October
SEED TREATMENT: Scarification. Soak 30 minutes in water 135°F. Glossy seeds must be free of other plant parts and must be planted immediately after being soaked. Seeds that sink probably will germinate; floaters have poor germination.
PROPAGATION: Best propagated from seed. To produce transplants, sow treated seed slightly more than ¼ inch deep, spaced at 2-inch intervals in a transplant area or in flats in a greenhouse. Greenhouse seedlings should be transplanted outdoors when about 3 inches in height, root-pruned, and replanted 6 to 7 inches apart in midsummer (July 15 to August 1 in Wisconsin). For permanent establishment, plant 1-year-old transplants in fall or early spring. If seed is used, it should be handplanted in spring after being treated with hot water.
COMPANION PLANTS: Thimbleweed; Butterfly Weed; Leadplant; Spiderwort; Little Bluestem
COMMENT: New Jersey tea is a pretty shrub, usually found in small groups with individual plants closely spaced. Old plants have a brittle, deeply branched taproot. The foliage has a subtle scent, is attractive to deer, and was used for tea in Revolutionary War times.

× 1   Color photograph, p. 36

Coreopsis palmata

COMMON NAMES: Stiff Coreopsis; Stiff Tickseed
KIND OF PRAIRIE: Dry; Mesic
HEIGHT: 1 to 3 feet
COLOR OF FLOWER: Yellow
FLOWERING TIME: June to mid-August: from transplants, the first year; from seed, the second year
SEED COLLECTION DATE: October to November
SEED TREATMENT: Dry stratification
PROPAGATION: Easily propagated by division of adult plants. Can also cut mature rhizomes into 2-inch sections, treat with Rootone, and plant horizontally 1 inch deep. Rhizomes with a well-developed bud on the tip form new plants rapidly. For permanent plantings, transplants can be established in either fall or spring. Plants are so easily divided and transplanted that seeding is not worthwhile. However, if seed is used, sow unstratified seed in fall, stratified seed in spring.
COMPANION PLANTS: Leadplant; Butterfly Weed; Rough Blazingstar; Western Sunflower; Flowering Spurge
COMMENT: The colorful flowers of this plant are often seen along roadsides. To limit spreading it is best kept on poor or light soils.

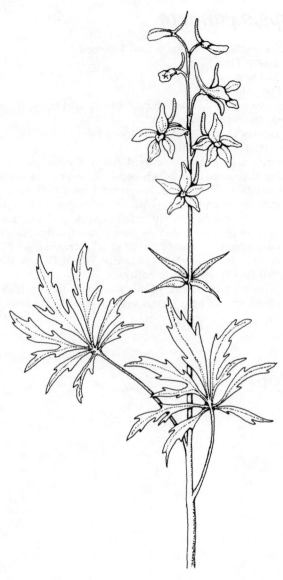

× ½   Color photograph, p. 36

Delphinium virescens

COMMON NAMES: Prairie Larkspur; Larksheel
KIND OF PRAIRIE: Dry; Mesic
HEIGHT: 1 to 3 feet
COLOR OF FLOWER: White with greenish or bluish tinge
FLOWERING TIME: June to late July: from transplants, the first year; from seed, the second year
SEED COLLECTION DATE: Variable
SEED TREATMENT: Fresh or dry stratification
PROPAGATION: Easily propagated from seed or by division. To produce transplants, either divide adult plants or sow fresh seed ¼ inch deep in early August or dry stratified seed in May. Seed apparently germinates best in cool weather and tends to wait for ideal conditions; this may be weeks or months. For permanent plantings, sow dry stratified seed in spring or use transplants in spring or fall.
COMPANION PLANTS: Little Bluestem; Sideoats; Junegrass; Purple Prairie Clover
COMMENT: Mature plants may for their own reasons disappear in hot weather for several months, then reappear in cool weather after all hope of regenerating is gone. All parts of fresh plants are poisonous, except to sheep. Early botanists thought the spur of this plant resembled the spur at the foot of a lark; thus, "larkspur." It was reputed to be used as a narcotic by early Native Americans.

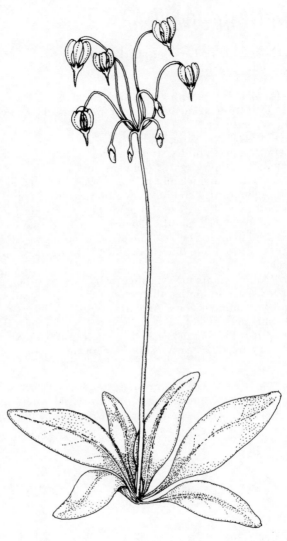

$\times$ ½   Color photograph, p. 36

Dodecatheon meadia

COMMON NAMES: Shootingstar; Indianchief; Pride-of-Ohio; American
Cowslip

KIND OF PRAIRIE: Dry; Mesic; Wet

HEIGHT: 1 to 2 feet

COLOR OF FLOWER: White, pale pink

FLOWERING TIME: May to early June: from transplants, the first or second year; from seed, the fourth or fifth year

SEED COLLECTION DATE: July

SEED TREATMENT: Moist or dry stratification, or fresh seed

PROPAGATION: Best propagated by division. Very fine seed germinates
well, but seedlings cannot be easily handled until the third or fourth
year because of their extremely slow growth. Young plants grow in
spring for a short time, but by July are dormant until the following
spring. Preliminary evidence indicates that chilling young plants for
10 days at 35°F before replanting in mid or late July increases growth
the following spring. To produce transplants, divide adult plants,
using a knife to cut the crown so each section has a root and a bud.
It is best to dig mature crowns in July when dormant; then divide,
and replant. Location must be labeled because plant is invisible during much of the growing season. On permanent sites, plant crowns
in early spring, in July, or in fall. With the right habitat and companions, seeding is possible, but slow.

COMPANION PLANTS: Little Bluestem; Purple Prairie Clover; Prairie
Phlox; Dwarf Blazingstar

COMMENT: This lovely pale star grows better and is easier to handle in
light sandy soil. It is often found in old cemeteries where spring sunlight is available. Seed pods are cuplike with tiny jagged edges.

× ¾   Color photograph, p. 37

Echinacea pallida

COMMON NAME: Pale Purple Coneflower
KIND OF PRAIRIE: Dry; Mesic
HEIGHT: 2 to 3 feet
COLOR OF FLOWER: Rosy purple
FLOWERING TIME: Late June to mid-July: from transplants, the second year; from seed, the second or third year
SEED COLLECTION DATE: October to November
SEED TREATMENT: Moist stratification improves germination.
PROPAGATION: Easily propagated from seed or by division. Often, however, division apparently stimulates the development of too many stems, thus resulting in a very bushy plant with a limited number of flowers. Seed produces more uniform transplants. Sow ¼ inch deep in spring (early June in Wisconsin). For permanent plantings, use seed or transplants in spring or fall. Small bits of root often sprout.
COMPANION PLANTS: Big Bluestem; Flowering Spurge; Yellow Coneflower; Rigid Goldenrod
COMMENT: This is an aggressive plant with coarse foliage. Like many members of the Daisy family, it shows off best when mixed with grasses. It has a long period of bloom and mixes well in fresh floral arrangements.

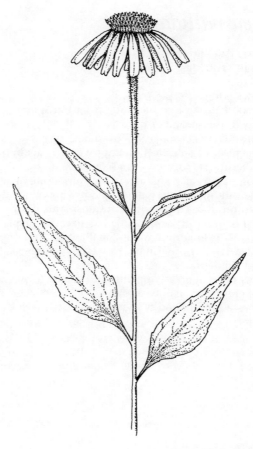

× ¼   Color photograph, p. 37

Echinacea purpurea

COMMON NAME: Purple Coneflower
KIND OF PRAIRIE: Dry
HEIGHT: 2 to 4 feet
COLOR OF FLOWER: Deep reddish purple with orange center disk
FLOWERING TIME: Late July to September: from seed, the second year,
SEED COLLECTION DATE: Late October
SEED TREATMENT: Moist stratification improves germination.
PROPAGATION: Best propagated from seed. Seed is enclosed in a tough, spiny head, hard to break. (I use a small hammermill.) Under natural conditions the seedhead falls to the ground, decomposes, and releases its seed. To produce transplants, sow seed slightly deeper than ¼ inch in spring (from early to late June in Wisconsin). Division is possible, but it does not produce high-quality transplants. They have too many stems, resulting in very bushy plants with a limited number of flowers. For permanent plantings use seed or 1-year-old transplants in fall or spring.
COMPANION PLANTS: Big Bluestem; Flowering Spurge; Yellow Coneflower; Rigid Goldenrod
COMMENT: Large, colorful flower blooms for 6 weeks. Plant grows well on very dry sand with a little mulch. It is strong seeder that quickly establishes itself. Because it is very aggressive, care should be exercised in its placement. It is limited in distribution; and in many areas, domesticated. It is a lovely, long-lasting addition to bouquets.

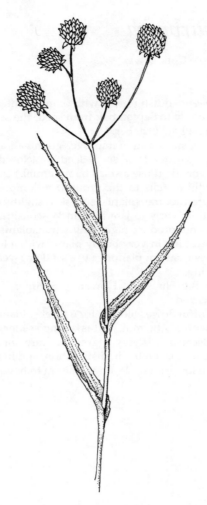

$\times \; \frac{1}{3}$ Color photograph, p. 37

Eryngium yuccifolium

COMMON NAMES: Rattlesnake Master; Snakeroot
KIND OF PRAIRIE: Dry; Mesic
HEIGHT: 3 to 4 feet
COLOR OF FLOWER: White blossoms, green spiny fruiting balls
FLOWERING TIME: Mid-July to mid-August: from transplants, the first year
SEED COLLECTION DATE: October
PROPAGATION: Easily propagated by division. To produce transplants, divide mature plants in spring or fall. To establish on permanent sites, use transplants in spring or fall.
COMPANION PLANTS: Big Bluestem; Heath Aster; Flowering Spurge; Bush Clover
COMMENT: This is an interesting plant with yucca-like leaves and an unusual seedhead, but an agressive seeder. Limit the number of plants and exercise caution in its use. Remove seed so additional plants are not produced willy-nilly. Brewed root was once drunk as an antidote to rattlesnake poison.

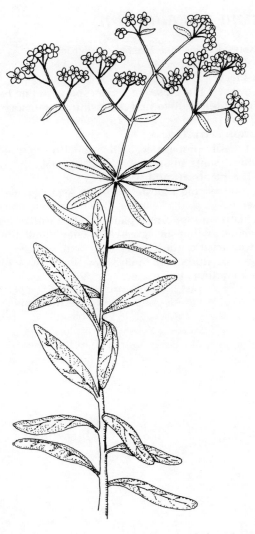

$\times$ ½   Color photograph, p. 37

Euphorbia corollata

COMMON NAMES: Flowering Spurge; Appleroot;'Purging Root; White Purslane; Milk Ipecac; Snake Milk; Wild Hippo
KIND OF PRAIRIE: Dry; Mesic
HEIGHT: 1 to 3 feet
COLOR OF FLOWER: Tiny white flowers. (Bright green leaves.)
FLOWERING TIME: June to September: from root cuttings, the first year; from seed, the second year
SEED COLLECTION DATE: Early September (seedhead explodes)
SEED TREATMENT: Moist stratification
PROPAGATION: Best propagated from seed. Roots are brittle; thus it is difficult to produce uniform transplants. For permanent establishment, use a 2- to 3-inch section of upper root containing buds as a transplant. Can also use 2-inch root cuttings treated with Rootone and planted 2 inches deep. Or seed may be sown, unstratified in fall, stratified in spring.
COMPANION PLANTS: Big Bluestem; Little Bluestem; Butterfly Weed; Leadplant; Bush Clover
COMMENT: This plant provides color from June until September. Its delicate lines make it an attractive filler in fresh bouquets. The milky juice in the stem is acrid enough to raise blisters on tender skin, and was once used as a laxative. Recently, test plots of a *Euphorbia* species were found to yield the equivalent of 10 to 20 barrels of oil per acre.

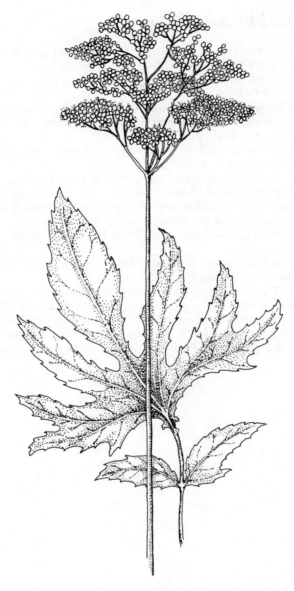

× ⅓   Color photograph, p. 37

Filipendula rubra

COMMON NAMES: Queen-of-the-Prairie; Prairie Meadowsweet

KIND OF PRAIRIE: Mesic; Wet

HEIGHT: 3 to 6 feet

COLOR OF FLOWER: Deep pink

FLOWERING TIME: July into August: from transplants, the first or second year

SEED COLLECTION DATE: August to September

PROPAGATION: Best propagated by division. Remove young plants produced by rhizomes alongside parent plants. Parent plants can be left in soil. If old plant is dug, remove rhizomes with terminal buds and treat with Rootone before planting.

COMPANION PLANTS: New England Aster; Joe-Pye Weed; Ironweed

COMMENT: This is a tall, regal plant with a spectacular bloom. Somewhat aggressive, it spreads by rhizomes. Its natural distribution is limited, but in many areas it is domesticated. It is said to have astringent properties because of its tannin content. Native Americans used it as a medicine to treat heart and love troubles.

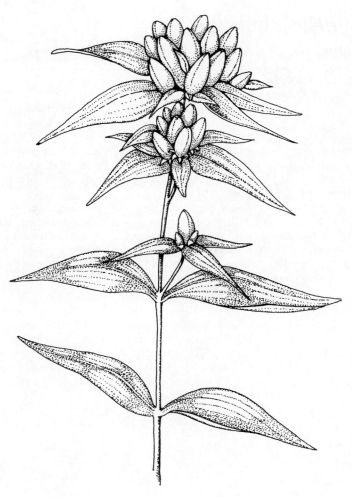

× ½   Color photograph, p. 38

Gentiana andrewsii

COMMON NAMES: Bottle Gentian; Blind Gentian; Cloistered Heart

KIND OF PRAIRIE: Mesic; Wet

HEIGHT: 1 to 2 feet

COLOR OF FLOWER: Deep brilliant blue

FLOWERING TIME: Early September to October: from transplants, the first year; from seed the fourth year

SEED COLLECTION DATE: October to November

SEED TREATMENT: Moist stratification for 10 days

PROPAGATION: Best propagated from seed, which germinates and grows very slowly the first year, faster thereafter. Can also be divided. To produce transplants, cover seeds lightly with soil in an area with partial shade. Seeds are very small. Seedlings need extensive protection the first year. It takes 2 years to produce strong transplants. To divide, cut so that each section has a root and a bud. For permanent plantings, use transplants in fall or spring. Repeated seeding in proper habitat over a 2- to 3-year period sometimes produces a number of plants.

COMPANION PLANTS: Big Bluestem; Turkscap; Prairie Phlox; New England Aster

COMMENT: This plant has beautiful deep blue blossoms that stay closed. Smooth green leaves form in pairs up the stalk. It does well and looks lovely in the average garden and in fresh or dried bouquets. Species named to honor Henry Andrews, a 19th-century botanical artist. Native Americans once made compresses from the roots and applied them to aching backs.

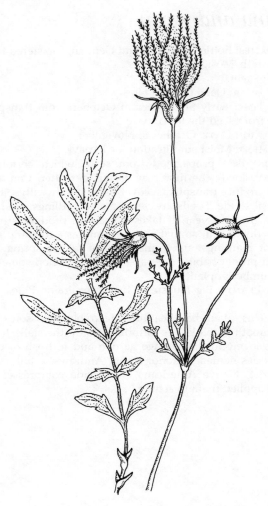

× 1   Color photograph, p. 38

Geum triflorum

COMMON NAMES: Prairie Smoke; Grandpa's Whiskers
KIND OF PRAIRIE: Dry; Mesic
HEIGHT: 8 to 14 inches
COLOR OF FLOWER: Deep rose
FLOWERING TIME: Late April to June: from division, the first year; from seed, the second year
SEED COLLECTION DATE: May to June
SEED TREATMENT: Dry stratification, or fresh seed
PROPAGATION: Can be propagated from seed or by division. To produce transplants, seeds should be sown in flats because they grow very slowly the first year. Remove seedlings from flats and transplant when leaves are 2 to 2½ inches long; division is easier. Separate transplants with light-colored roots from those with heavy black lateral roots. For permanent plantings, use transplants in early spring or fall. Including small sections of coarse old root on transplants will increase the chance of survival in dry areas. Adding a little lime also helps.
COMPANION PLANTS: Pasque Flower; Leadplant; Big Bluestem; Thimbleweed; Sideoats; Needlegrass
COMMENT: Growth is good in early spring and during cool fall weather. Feathery blossoms continue over a long period, and can be sprayed with hair spray for a dry bouquet. Mature plants frequently form dense mats, and are desirable near dwellings where other species may be too coarse.

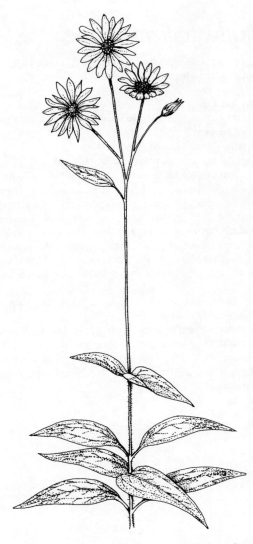

× ¼   Color photograph, p. 38

Helianthus occidentalis

COMMON NAMES: Western Sunflower; Sunflower
KIND OF PRAIRIE: Dry; Mesic
HEIGHT: 1 to 3 feet
COLOR OF FLOWER : Yellow
FLOWERING TIME: August to October: from division, the second year
SEED COLLECTION DATE: October to November
SEED TREATMENT: Dry stratification
PROPAGATION: Best propagated by division. To produce transplants, divide mature plants so that each division has a root and a leaf bud. Transplants can also be produced in one season from seeds sown ¼ inch deep in spring (early June in Wisconsin). On permanent sites, divided plants are easily established. Seed can be sown in spring or fall.
COMPANION PLANTS: Coreopsis; Birdsfoot Violet; Lupine; Prairie Rose; Rough Blazingstar; Flowering Spurge;
COMMENT: This plant has bright yellow blossoms in late summer and early fall. The generic name comes from the Greek words *helios*, sun, and *anthos*, flower. This golden beauty was worshipped by early Incas as a symbol of the sun. It is a typical dry sandy soil plant that spreads rapidly if moisture is added and soil is fertilized.

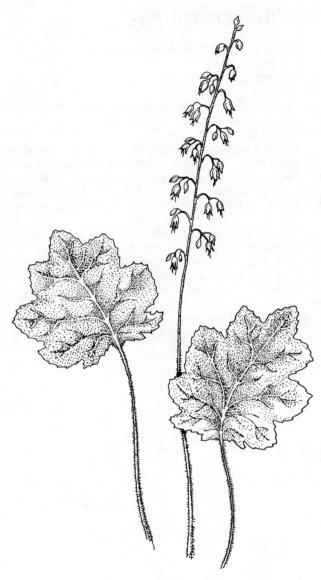

× ½   Color photograph, p. 38

Heuchera richardsonii

COMMON NAME: Alumroot
KIND OF PRAIRIE: Dry; Mesic; Wet
HEIGHT: 1 to 2 feet
COLOR OF FLOWER: Greenish white
FLOWERING TIME: May to June: from division, the first year; from seed, the second year
SEED COLLECTION DATE: Late June to July
SEED TREATMENT: Fresh seed, or dry stratification
PROPAGATION: Best propagated from seed; can also be divided. To produce transplants, sow seed in flats in a greenhouse or in a protected outdoor area. Seeds are very tiny and should be planted on the surface of the soil. They need light to germinate. Because seed is so small, it is very easy to sow too many; under greenhouse conditions this may lead to damping off. Use a sharp knife to divide mature plants after they have produced their seed in midsummer, and make sure to get a root section with buds. For permanent plantings, use transplants in fall or spring, although seeding is a possibility
COMPANION PLANTS: Shootingstar; Prairie Phlox; Columbine; Flowering Spurge
COMMENT: Small, spikelike flower clusters and attractive green foliage complement companion plants adjacent to buildings. The rounded root of this plant was used by early Native Americans as a poultice and an antiseptic. Reportedly, the juice was also used in 17th-century England for secret writing.

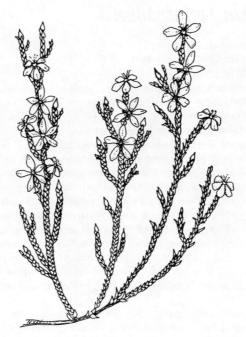

× 1   Color photograph, p. 39

Hudsonia tomentosa

COMMON NAME: False heather
KIND OF PRAIRIE: Dry sandblows
HEIGHT: 4 to 12 inches
COLOR OF FLOWER: Small yellow flower. (Steel-blue needled foliage.)
FLOWERING TIME: June
PROPAGATION: I have not propagated this plant. But I have been successful transplanting and extending its range in sandblows where it already existed. It propagates naturally from seed, spreading in bushy patches, although rate of increase is slow.
COMPANION PLANTS: Little Bluestem; Frostweed; Bush Clover; Puccoon
COMMENT: This plant has prostrate growth; its hard tough leaves resemble heather. A member of the Rockrose family, it is not usually classified as a prairie plant. A good soil stabilizer, it is common on sandblows and has been called the "prize of all beach plants."

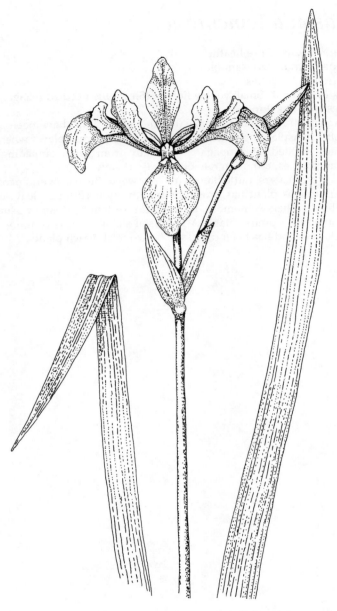

× 1   Color photograph, p. 39

Iris shrevei

COMMON NAMES: Wild Iris; Blue Flag
KIND OF PRAIRIE: Mesic; Wet
HEIGHT: 1 to 3 feet
COLOR OF FLOWER: Blue-violet
FLOWERING TIME: May to July: from division, the first or second year
SEED COLLECTION DATE: September
SEED TREATMENT: Fresh
PROPAGATION: Best propagated by division. To produce transplants, divide mature plants in spring or fall, or in mid-summer after blooming. Fertilization of older plants will encourage new shoots. On permanent locations, use transplants in spring or fall.
COMPANION PLANTS: Swamp Milkweed; Boneset; Joe-Pye Weed
COMMENT: This is a colorful beauty; *iris* in Greek means rainbow. It grows very well in average garden soil and in favorable habitat spreads rapidly from large rhizomes. Its rhizomes were once used as a cathartic, and can cause severe digestive upset.

× ½   Color photograph, p. 39

Lespedeza capitata (A legume)

COMMON NAMES: Bush Clover; Rabbitfoot; Roundhead Lespedeza
KIND OF PRAIRIE: Dry; Mesic
HEIGHT: 2 to 3 feet
COLOR OF FLOWER: Creamy white
FLOWERING TIME: August and September: from seed, the second year
SEED COLLECTION DATE: October to November
SEED TREATMENT: Scarification, moist stratification for 10 days
PROPAGATION: Easily propagated from seed. Seeds sown ¼ inch deep will produce transplant stock in one season. For permanent plantings, sow unstratified seed in fall or stratified seed in spring. Transplants can also be used in fall or spring.
COMPANION PLANTS: Little Bluestem; Leadplant; Junegrass; Western Sunflower; Coreopsis; Lupine
COMMENT: This pioneer grows easily and abundantly on dry prairies and abandoned farm fields, but not as well on mesic prairies. Being a legume, it paves the way for other prairie plants by improving soil nitrogen. Livestock like it. Its seed provides food for gamebirds and other wildlife. Its seedhead is an attractive filler in dried bouquets. Its taproot extends 5 to 8 feet and apparently is indestructible. Sprouts can be grown in flats and eaten like alfalfa or bean sprouts. This legume is a very satisfactory addition to any prairie planting, but tends to decrease in numbers in undisturbed areas.

× ½   Color photograph, p. 39

Liatris aspera

COMMON NAMES: Rough Blazingstar; Gayfeather; Colicroot; Devil's
Bite; Rattlesnake Master; Snakeroot

KIND OF PRAIRIE: Dry; Mesic

HEIGHT: 2 to 4 feet

COLOR OF FLOWER: Bright magenta-purple flowers, smooth white or
pink bracts

FLOWERING TIME: August to September: from corms, the first year;
from seed, the second or third year

SEED COLLECTION DATE: October

SEED TREATMENT: Dry stratification

PROPAGATION: Best propagated from seed. Seed sown ¼ inch deep in
June will produce small corms suitable for transplanting in one season. Old corms can be divided, using a sharp knife, so that each
division receives a bud and a root section. If divisions are transplanted in fall, treat with gladiola dust to prevent rotting. For permanent plantings, sow unstratified seed in fall, stratified seed in
spring. Transplanted corms should be covered with at least 2½
inches of soil.

COMPANION PLANTS: Bushclover; Junegrass; Little Bluestem; Yellow
Coneflower; Purple Prairie Clover. (Needs companion plants to prevent lodging.)

COMMENT: This is an excellent plant for dry areas. Sometimes in sand
country it dominates all competition. On such occasions the bright
blossoms make a spectacular display. *Liatris aspera* is one of the 20 or
so species of *Liatris* in North America. Grasslike leaves help conserve
water. Corms, which enlarge with age, store water and nutrients,
and once were dug and kept for winter meals. Tea was made from
the leaves to treat stomachaches and snakebites.

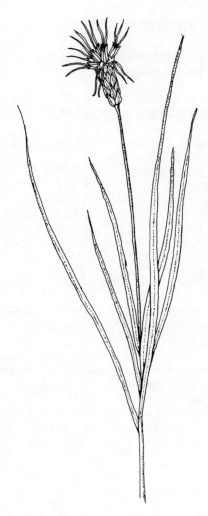

$\times$ 1   Color photograph, p. 40

Liatris cylindracea

COMMON NAMES: Dwarf Blazingstar; Button Snakeroot; Gayfeather
KIND OF PRAIRIE: Dry
HEIGHT: 1 to 2 feet
COLOR OF FLOWER: Bright purple flowers, flat green bracts
FLOWERING TIME: Mid-July to end of August: from seed, the second or third year
SEED COLLECTION DATE: September to October
SEED TREATMENT: Dry stratification
PROPAGATION: Best propagated from seed. Seed sown ¼ inch deep in June will produce small corms suitable for transplanting in one season. Use a sharp knife to divide old corms so that each division has a bud and a root section. If corms are transplanted in fall, treat with gladiola dust to prevent rotting. For permanent plantings, sow unstratified seed in fall, stratified seed in spring. Transplant corms and divisions also can be used in fall or spring. Corms should be covered with at least 2½ inches of soil.
COMPANION PLANTS: Sideoats; Coreopsis; Junegrass; Prairie Dropseed; Pasque Flower; Needlegrass; Little Bluestem; Purple Prairie Clover
COMMENT: This bright bloom is eye-catching in a prairie landscape. Volunteer seedlings are abundant; seeds are easy to collect in fall. The blossoms are a common sight in remnant limestone prairies.

× ½   Color photograph, p. 40

Liatris pycnostachya

COMMON NAMES: Prairie Blazingstar; Gayfeather; Rattlesnake Master
KIND OF Prairie: Mesic; Wet
HEIGHT: 2 to 4 feet
COLOR OF FLOWER: Bright magenta-purple flowers, hairy pink bracts
FLOWERING TIME: Mid-July to early August: from transplants, the first year; from seed, the second year
SEED COLLECTION DATE: September to October
SEED TREATMENT: Moist stratification
PROPAGATION: Best propagated from seed. Seed sown ¼ inch deep in June will produce small corms suitable for transplanting in one season. Old corms can be divided with a sharp knife. If cut divisions are transplanted in fall, treat with gladiola dust to prevent rotting. For permanent plantings, sow unstratified seed in fall, stratified seed in spring. Transplant corms and divisions can be used in fall or spring. Corms should be covered with at least 2½ inches of soil.
COMPANION PLANTS: Big Bluestem; Shootingstar; Turkscap; Yellow Coneflower; Stiff Goldenrod; Spiderwort; Culversroot; Little Bluestem. (Tends to lodge, needs companion plants to prevent it.)
COMMENT: Spectacular spikes bloom in top-down order with varying flowering periods, thus prolonging the flowering season. Blooms before dwarf blazingstar or rough blazingstar. Flowers are magnificent in fresh arrangements, and hold color well in dried bouquets if picked at their peak and kept out of the sun. Tubers were once used to treat rattlesnake bites.

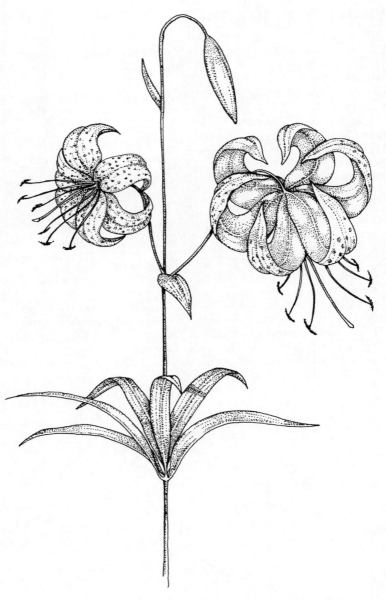

$\times$ ½   Color photograph, p. 40

Lilium superbum

COMMON NAME: Turkscap
KIND OF PRAIRIE: Wet; Mesic
HEIGHT: 2 to 4 feet
COLOR OF FLOWER: Spotted reddish orange
FLOWERING TIME: Late June to August: from scales, the second year
SEED COLLECTION DATE: September
SEED TREATMENT: Needs none.
PROPAGATION: Best propagated from bulb scales (division). To produce transplants, separate scales from central core of bulb and plant 1 inch deep; can also plant core. Transplanting is best in fall. Much of the development occurs underground, with little showing on the surface the first year. Two years are required to produce transplant stock. On permanent sites, transplant mature bulbs 2 inches deep or scales and cores 1 inch deep in fall or early spring. It is also possible to sow seed ½ inch deep, but it will take at least another year to bloom.
COMPANION PLANTS: Big Bluestem; Bergamot; Wild Iris; Culversroot; Bottle Gentian. (Needs companion plants close by to prevent lodging.)
COMMENT: This flame-colored beauty is a stand-out among its companions, particularly if planted in colonies. Within a few years a single plant will produce rhizomes and new bulbs, and, of course, new clusters of flowers. The flowers are sometimes confused with those of *Lilium michiganense*, which are larger and lighter colored.

× 1   Color photograph, p. 40

Lithospermum croceum

COMMON NAMES: Hairy Puccoon; Puccoon
KIND OF PRAIRIE: Dry; Mesic
HEIGHT: 8 to 10 inches
COLOR OF FLOWER: Golden yellow
FLOWERING TIME: May to June: from cuttings, the second year
SEED COLLECTION DATE: July
SEED TREATMENT: On the basis of limited experience I suggest soaking
seed in hot water 135°F; plant immediately.
PROPAGATION: Best propagated from 2-inch root cuttings. To produce
transplants, treat cuttings with Rootone and plant right side up, 2
inches deep, in fall. For permanent establishment, use the root cut-
tings.
COMPANION PLANTS: Lupine; Flowering Spurge; Big Bluestem; Sideoats; Bush Clover
COMMENT: *Puccoon* is the Native American word given to dye-yielding
plants. Steeped roots yield purplish dye. Generic name is from the
Greek words *lethos*, stone, and *sperma*, seed. Native Americans are
said to have used the plant as an oral contraceptive.

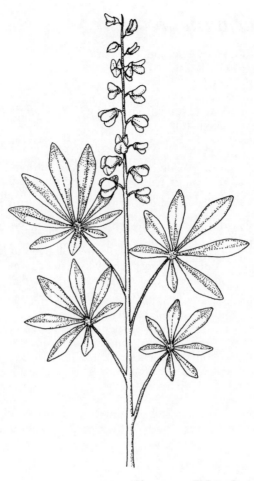

× ½   Color photograph, p. 40

Lupinus perennis (A legume)

COMMON NAME: Lupine
KIND OF PRAIRIE: Dry; Mesic
HEIGHT: 10 to 18 inches
COLOR OF FLOWER: Blue-violet to pink to white
FLOWERING TIME: Late May to June: from seed, the second year
SEED COLLECTION DATE: Late June to early July. (Seedhead explodes.)
SEED TREATMENT: Fresh seed from pod can be inoculated and planted
immediately. Dry seed best. Scarification, inoculation, moist stratifi-
cation for 10 days.
PROPAGATION: Easily propagated from seed. To produce transplants,
sow seed ¾ inch deep in spring or fall. Seedlings grow rapidly and
should be transplanted when they get their first true leaves and
when roots are from 6 to 8 inches long. On permanent sites, sow
unstratified seed in fall; stratified seed in spring. A hand corn-planter
may be used, but seed must not be planted deeper than ¾ inch.
Transplants can also be used.
COMPANION PLANTS: Leadplant, Coreopsis; Western Sunflower; Prairie
Smoke; Birdsfoot Violet; Big Bluestem (but does not like heavy grass
competition); Butterfly Weed; Flowering Spurge
COMMENT: There are 200 or more species of this lovely legume in North
America. Arctic lupine seeds recently found cached in a lemming
burrow in the Yukon had been frozen for 10,000 years. After being
sown, they germinated within 48 hours, thus causing scientists to
ponder whether the long freeze brought about the early germination.
The generic name is from the Latin *lupus*, wolf, because the plant
was once thought to rob soil of nutrients. Instead it is an excellent
soil-builder. All parts are believed to be poisonous if eaten.

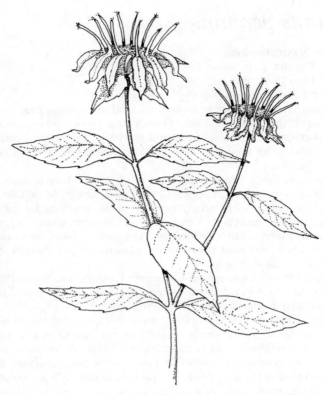

× ¾   Color photograph, p. 40

Monarda fistulosa

COMMON NAMES: Bergamot; Horsemint; Bee Balm
KIND OF PRAIRIE: Dry; Mesic; Wet
HEIGHT: 2 to 3 feet
COLOR OF FLOWER: Lavender
FLOWERING TIME: Early July to August: from seed, the second year
SEED COLLECTION DATE: August to September
SEED TREATMENT: Moist stratification improves germination.
PROPAGATION: Easily propagated from seed. Seed sown ¼ inch deep in spring (early June in Wisconsin) will produce transplants in one season. Mature plants can also be divided, but heavy growth of rhizomes makes division difficult. On permanent sites, sow unstratified seed in fall, stratified seed in spring. One-year-old transplants can also be used.
COMPANION PLANTS: Yellow Coneflower; Big Bluestem; Turkscap; Culversroot
COMMENT: This shaggy, fragrant member of the Mint family is apparently distasteful to plant-eating insects. Common along roadsides in Wisconsin, it needs competition to control its spreading in prairie landscapes. Attractive solid clumps can be encouraged by mulching. Leaves make strong tea said to be soothing to an upset stomach. Generic name honors Nicolas Monardes, a 16th-century Spanish physician and horticulturalist.

×1   Color photograph, p. 41

Monarda punctata

COMMON NAMES: Dotted Mint; Horsemint; Spotted Bee Balm

KIND OF PRAIRIE: Dry

HEIGHT: 8 to 18 inches

COLOR OF FLOWER: Yellow cream, spotted, purple, set off by conspicuous white or lilac bracts beneath each cluster

FLOWERING TIME: July to September: from transplants, the first year; from seed, the second year

SEED COLLECTION DATE: September to October

SEED TREATMENT: Moist or dry stratification

PROPAGATION: Easily propagated from seed. Seed sown ¼ inch deep in spring (early June in Wisconsin) will produce transplants in one season. On permanent sites, sow unstratified seed in fall, stratified seed in spring. Transplants can also be used in fall or spring.

COMPANION PLANTS: Junegrass; Western Sunflower; Lupine; Leadplant; Big Bluestem; Little Bluestem; Butterfly Weed

COMMENT: This aggressive plant will quickly take over abandoned agricultural fields in sand country. On dewy mornings, it is beautiful in masses. Its seed can be stored in the soil for long periods. Its dried powdered leaves, flowers, and stalks once were used as a headache snuff. Fresh or dried leaves can be made into tea or used for flavoring.

×½   Color photograph, p. 41

Oenothera biennis

COMMON NAMES: Evening Primrose; Night Willow Herb; Coffee Plant;
  Fever Plant; King's Cure-all
KIND OF PRAIRIE; Dry; Mesic
HEIGHT: 1 to 2 feet
COLOR OF FLOWER: Yellow
FLOWERING TIME: July to mid-September: from seed, the second year
SEED COLLECTION DATE: August to November
SEED TREATMENT: Dry stratification
PROPAGATION: Easily propagated from seed. Sow unstratified seed ¼
  inch deep in fall, stratified seed in spring. Does well the first few
  years in newly established prairie landscapes, but does not persist as
  more long-lived perennials take hold. Seed stays, however, and germinates if soil is disturbed.
COMPANION PLANTS: Flowering Spurge; Dotted Mint; Bush Clover
COMMENT: Attractive, delicate flowers open in the evening air and
  close the following morning. This plant is generally found in abandoned fields, roadsides, and waste places, and is a staple food of
  goldfinches. Leaves can be eaten as cooked greens. Boiled roots taste
  like parsnips and supposedly increase a person's wine-drinking capacity.

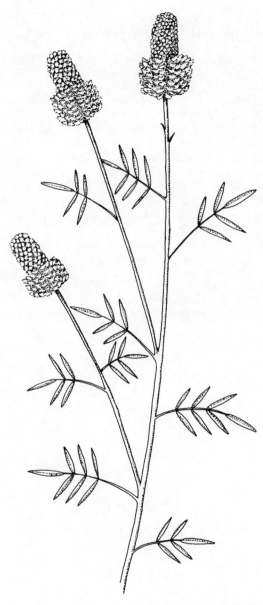

$\times\ \frac{1}{2}$ Color photograph, p. 41

Petalostemum candidum (A legume)

COMMON NAME: White Prairie Clover
KIND OF PRAIRIE: Dry; Mesic
HEIGHT: 1 to 3 feet
COLOR OF FLOWER: White
FLOWERING TIME: July to mid-August: from seed, the second year
SEED COLLECTION DATE: August to September
SEED TREATMENT: Scarification, inoculation, moist stratification for 10 days
PROPAGATION: Easily propagated from seed. Seed sown ¼ inch deep in spring (early June in Wisconsin) will produce good-sized transplants in one season. On permanent sites, sow unstratified seed in fall, stratified seed in spring. One-year-old transplants can also be used in fall or spring.
COMPANION PLANTS: Sideoats; Leadplant; Butterfly Weed
COMMENT: Attractive flowerheads rise above surrounding grasses. Petals and stamens are joined. Leafy portions are tasty to cottontails. The deep taproot, pulverized, makes fine-tasting tea.

× ½   Color photograph, p. 41

Petalostemum purpureum (A legume)

COMMON NAMES: Purple Prairie Clover; Violet Prairie Clover; Red Tassel Flower

KIND OF PRAIRIE: Dry; Mesic

HEIGHT: 1 to 3 feet

COLOR OF FLOWER: Purple

FLOWERING TIME: July to mid-August: from seed, the second year

SEED COLLECTION DATE: August to September

SEED TREATMENT: Scarification, inoculation, moist stratification for 10 days

PROPAGATION: Easily propagated from seed. Seed sown ¼ inch deep in spring (June in Wisconsin) will produce transplants in one season. For permanent plantings, sow unstratified seed in fall, stratified seed in spring. One-year-old transplants also do well planted in either fall or spring.

COMPANION PLANTS: Thimbleweed; Sideoats; Flowering Spurge; Bush Clover; Rough Blazingstar; Little Bluestem

COMMENT: Many stems of this legume grow from a single base. Its lovely flower and foilage, for some reason, are not as attractive to rabbits as are those of white prairie clover. Tea made from vigorous taproot is said to reduce fever in measles victims. Sprouts are tasty, but very small.

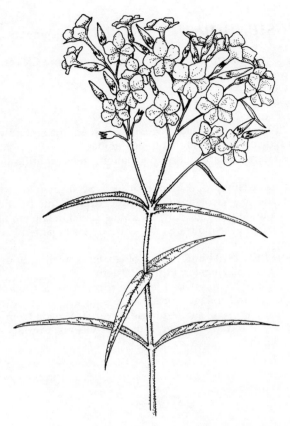

× ½   Color photograph, p. 42

Phlox pilosa

COMMON NAMES: Prairie Phlox; Downy Phlox
KIND OF PRAIRIE: Dry; Mesic; Wet
HEIGHT: 1 to 2 feet
COLOR OF FLOWER: Purplish rose, sometimes white
FLOWERING TIME: May and June: from cuttings, the first or second year; from seed, the second year
SEED COLLECTION DATE: July. (Seedhead explodes.)
SEED TREATMENT: Moist stratification until seed shows early signs of germination
PROPAGATION: Best propagated from stem cuttings. Seed is unpredictable, averaging 2 out of 6 successful germinations. To produce transplants, treat 6-inch stem cuttings with Rootone and for best results, plant 2 to 4 inches deep in rooting medium, such as sand or a prepared mixture of peat and sand. Cuttings should be started in flats and moved when they achieve good leaf and root development. For permanent plantings, use transplants or sow unstratified seed in fall, stratified seed in spring.
COMPANION PLANTS: Shootingstar; Alumroot; Blackeyed Susan; Flowering Spurge; Spiderwort
COMMENT: The name *phlox* is from the Greek, meaning flame. The bright color of this plant enhances any prairie planting, small or large, near or far from dwellings. The many species and varieties range from Quebec to Florida and Texas. Flowers were once used for medicinal purposes.

× 1 Color photograph, p. 42 Color photograph, p. 42

Psoralea esculenta (A legume)

COMMON NAMES: Prairie Turnip; Scurfpea
KIND OF PRAIRIE: Dry
HEIGHT: 10 to 14 inches
COLOR OF FLOWER: Bluish
FLOWERING TIME: Mid-May to mid-June: from seed, the third year
SEED COLLECTION DATE: September
SEED TREATMENT: Scarification, inoculation, moist stratification for 10 days
PROPAGATION: Easily propagated from seed that resembles a small black bean. Seed sown ¼ inch deep in spring will produce a 10-inch root by fall. For permanent plantings, sow unstratified seed in fall, stratified seed in spring. (Transplanted 1-year-old stock should also be satisfactory, but I have had no experience moving this plant.)
COMPANION PLANTS: Purple Prairie Clover; Sideoats; Needlegrass
COMMENT: This plant is rather rare in Wisconsin, but common farther west. Flower is modest. Foliage is similar to lupine, but stiff and dusty in color. Root is edible. John C. Fremont was impressed in 1842 by the sight of Native Americans in Kansas digging these "prairie potatoes."

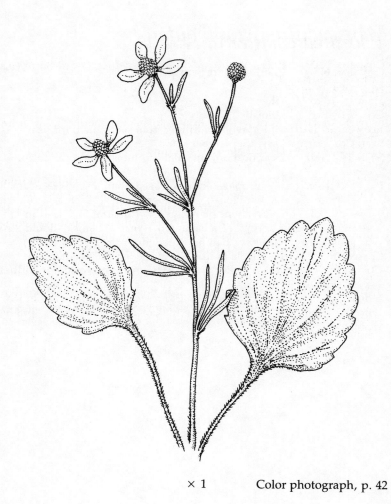

× 1   Color photograph, p. 42

Ranunculus rhomboideus

COMMON NAMES: Prairie Buttercup; Prairie Crowfoot; Dwarf Buttercup
KIND OF PRAIRIE: Dry
HEIGHT: 3 to 10 inches
COLOR OF FLOWER: Glossy yellow
FLOWERING TIME: April to May: from transplants, the first year; from seed, the second year
SEED COLLECTION DATE: Late May and June
SEED TREATMENT: Fresh seed
PROPAGATION: Best propagated from seed. Fresh seed planted in June emerges in mid-August. The tiny plants, some only 3 to 4 inches high, flower the following spring. To produce transplants, sow seeds as soon as collected, ⅛ inch deep. Water periodically until germination. For permanent plantings, use transplants in fall or very early spring. Seeds may be used, but have low germination.
COMPANION PLANTS: Alumroot; Prairie Phlox; Flowering Spurge; Rough Blazingstar
COMMENT: Colonies of this small, hardy buttercup have been known to persist even in quack sod. They look well in rock gardens and as border plants. American settlers used the roots of several species to stop nosebleeds.

144   × ½   Color photograph, p. 42

Ratibida pinnata

COMMON NAMES: Yellow Coneflower; Prairie Coneflower; Grayheaded Coneflower

KIND OF PRAIRIE: Dry; Mesic; Wet

HEIGHT: 3 to 5 feet

COLOR OF FLOWER: Yellow with gray cone that darkens with maturity

FLOWERING TIME: July to August: from seed, the second year

SEED COLLECTION DATE: October to November

SEED TREATMENT: Moist stratification improves germination.

PROPAGATION: Easily propagated from seed. Seed sown ¼ inch deep in spring will produce transplanting stock by fall. Mature plants can be divided, but division is difficult because of extensive fibrous root system. On permanent sites, use transplants or sow unstratified seed in fall or stratified seed in spring.

COMPANION PLANTS: Big Bluestem; Leadplant; Flowering Spurge; Bushclover

COMMENT: This major midsummer bloomer is showy, tall, and aggressive. It needs competition, particularly in small areas. Flower lends itself to any type of cut arrangement, and holds up beautifully.

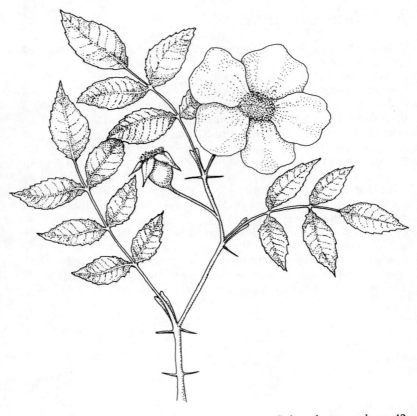

× 1 Color photograph, p. 42

Rosa sp.

COMMON NAMES: Prairie Rose; Wild Rose; Meadow Rose; Pasture Rose

KIND OF PRAIRIE: Dry; Mesic

HEIGHT: 1 to 3 feet

COLOR OF FLOWER: Crimson to faded pink to white with gold stamens at center

FLOWERING TIME: Late May to July: from cuttings, the second year

PROPAGATION: Best propagated from stem cuttings or division of root stock. To produce transplants, cut 6-inch green wood stems in July, treat with Rootone, plant 2 to 3 inches deep in rooting medium, such as sand or a prepared mixture of peat and sand. Flats are recommended. On permanent sites, transplant 1-year-old root cuttings or mature divided plants. (Seed is slow to germinate.)

COMPANION PLANTS: Flowering Spurge; Birdsfoot Violet; Western Sunflower

COMMENT: "A rose is a rose," lovely and fragrant, with its prickly thorns. Fat rose hips in fall make delicious jelly if seeds are strained out; they are high in vitamin C. Petals can be used in salads.

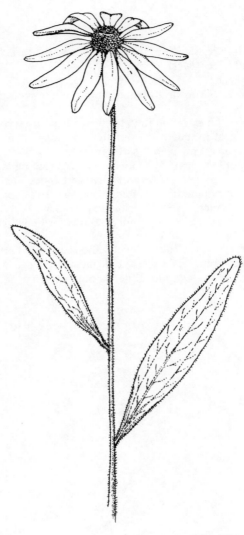

× ¾   Color photograph, p. 42

Rudbeckia hirta

COMMON NAMES: Blackeyed Susan; Yellow Daisy; Darkyhead; Poor-land Daisy; English Bull's-eye; Brown Betty

KIND OF PRAIRIE: Dry; Mesic; Wet

HEIGHT: 1 to 3 feet

COLOR OF FLOWER: Orange-yellow with deep brown center disk

FLOWERING TIME: July to August: from seed, the second year

SEED COLLECTION DATE: September to October

SEED TREATMENT: Moist stratification improves germination.

PROPAGATION: Easily propagated from seed. To produce transplants, sow seed ¼ inch deep in early July. (Seed sown in early spring produces transplants too large for easy handling.) For permanent plantings, sow unstratified seed in fall or stratified seed in early spring, or use transplants in fall or early spring. Seed or transplant 2 successive years; otherwise plants may bloom only every other year.

COMPANION PLANTS: Bush Clover; Flowering Spurge; Little Bluestem; Purple Prairie Clover; Spiderwort

COMMENT: This popular, adaptable member of the Daisy family has bristly leaves and stem. It is called both biennial and perennial, depending on site and geographic location. It is found on a variety of soils from Canada to the Gulf of Mexico and east on prairies throughout the United States. Its leaves were dried and steeped and used by early Americans as a kidney stimulant. Recent research indicates extracts have antibiotic properties. The generic name honors Olaf Rudbeck, a botanist from Sweden who lived just before Linnaeus, the great Swedish botanist who in the mid-18th century began the systematic plant classification we use today.

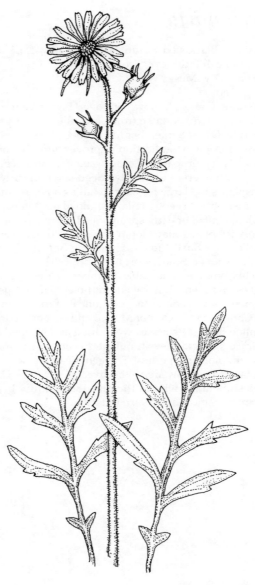

$\times$ ¼   Color photograph, p. 43

Silphium laciniatum

COMMON NAMES: Compassplant; Rosinweed; Pilotweed; Gumweed
KIND OF PRAIRIE: Dry; Mesic
HEIGHT: 4 to 8 feet
COLOR OF FLOWER: Yellow
FLOWERING TIME: Late June to August: from seed, the third to fifth year
SEED COLLECTION DATE: September to October
SEED TREATMENT: Moist stratification for 10 days
PROPAGATION: Easily propagated from seed. To produce transplants, sow seed ½ inch deep in late summer (about August 10 in Wisconsin) to avoid heavy growth of taproot. This will produce transplants for use in fall and very early spring. On permanent sites, sow unstratified seed in fall or stratified seed in early spring. Transplants can also be used in fall or very early spring.
COMPANION PLANTS: Big Bluestem; Purple Prairie Clover; Prairiedock; Rattlesnake Master; Yellow Coneflower
COMMENT: This classic prairie plant, resembling a sunflower, is aggressive and needs companion plants to keep it under control. The long-lived root of a mature plant can reach a depth of 15 feet or more. Coarse leaves often present edges to the sun; thus the name "compass." Grazing animals like it. Young Native Americans in early times chewed gum from an extract of the stem.

$\times \frac{1}{3}$ Color photograph, p. 43

152

Silphium perfoliatum

COMMON NAMES: Cupplant; Rosinweed; Indian Cup; Ragged Cup
KIND OF PRAIRIE: Mesic; Wet
HEIGHT: 3 to 6 feet
COLOR OF FLOWER: Yellow
FLOWERING TIME: July to September: from seed, the third year
SEED COLLECTION DATE: September to October
SEED TREATMENT: Moist stratification for 10 days
PROPAGATION: Easily propagated from seed. To produce transplants, sow seeds ½ inch deep in spring (early June in Wisconsin). Has spreading fibrous root. Plants up to 2 years old can be used as transplants. After that transplanting is too difficult. On permanent sites, use up to 2-year-old transplants in fall or spring. Or sow unstratified seed in fall or stratified seed in spring.
COMPANION PLANTS: Angelica; Joe-Pye Weed; Culversroot; Wild Iris
COMMENT: This plant is especially interesting, clumped in large areas. Stout joined leaves at stem form a small cup that holds water and attracts birds. Bright flowerheads are 2 to 3 inches across.

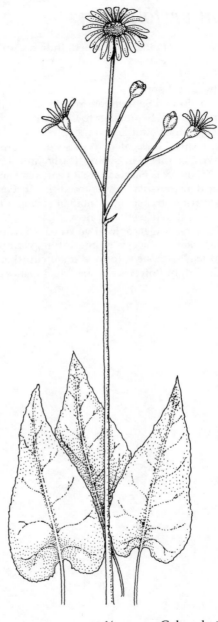

154   × ¼   Color photograph, p. 43

Silphium terebinthinaceum

COMMON NAMES: Prairiedock; Elephant Ear

KIND OF PRAIRIE: Mesic; Wet

HEIGHT: 3 to 6 feet

COLOR OF FLOWER: Yellow

FLOWERING TIME: July to September: from seed, the third or fourth year

SEED COLLECTION DATE: September to October

SEED TREATMENT: Moist stratification for 10 days

PROPAGATION: Easily propagated from seed. To produce transplants, sow seed ½ inch deep in late summer (about August 10 in Wisconsin). Late planting is necessary because of rapid growth of taproot and will produce transplant stock in fall and early following spring. On permanent sites, use transplants in fall or early spring, or sow unstratified seed in fall or stratified seed in spring.

COMPANION PLANTS: Big Bluestem; Alumroot; Bush Clover; White False Indigo; Prairie Phlox; Yellow Coneflower

COMMENT: This classic plant has large basal leaves; it is probably too coarse for most small prairie plantings. The steeped root of many *Silphium* species was used by early settlers for a variety of ailments, including so-called "female complaints."

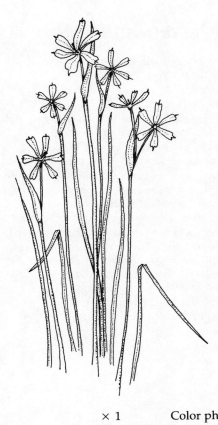

× 1   Color photograph, p. 43

Sisyrinchium campestre

COMMON NAMES: Blue-eyed Grass; Prairie Blue-eyed Grass
KIND OF PRAIRIE: Dry
HEIGHT: 8 to 10 inches
COLOR OF FLOWER: Deep blue, white, with a yellow eye
FLOWERING TIME: May to June: from division, the first year if divided in early spring; from seed, the second year
SEED COLLECTION DATE: July
SEED TREATMENT: Dry stratification, or fresh seed
PROPAGATION: Best propagated by division in early spring. Divide so that each section has several buds and roots. On permanent sites, transplant divisions in either fall or spring.
COMPANION PLANTS: Thimbleweed; Sideoats; Prairie Dropseed
COMMENT: This small, easy-to-manage member of the Iris family, with its grasslike leaves and starlike flowers, looks lovely and does well in sunny rock gardens, along paths, near dwellings, or any dry and sunlit area. It is said to have been one of Thoreau's favorite plants. The delicate flowers bloom only on sunny mornings, close upon being picked, and produce pea-sized seedheads that contain many tiny seeds.

× ¼   Color photograph, p. 44

Solidago nemoralis

COMMON NAME: Gray Goldenrod
KIND OF PRAIRIE: Dry
HEIGHT: 1 to 3 feet
COLOR OF FLOWER: Bright yellow-gold
FLOWERING TIME: August to October: from division, the first year; from seed, the second year
SEED COLLECTION DATE: October
SEED TREATMENT: Dry stratification
PROPAGATION: Easily propagated by division. Can also use seed. To produce transplants, divide mature plants so that each section has a bud and a root; sow seed ¼ inch deep in spring (early June in Wisconsin). On permanent sites, use transplants in fall or spring. Or sow unstratified seed in fall, stratified seed in spring.
COMPANION PLANTS: Leadplant; Flowering Spurge; Big Bluestem; Little Bluestem; Sideoats; Junegrass
COMMENT: Individual plants bloom at various times, thus extending the blooming season. *Solidago* species do not cause allergy problems; they bloom at the same time as ragweed, the real culprit. Their relatively heavy, harmless pollen grains are carried by flies, bees, butterflies, ants, and birds, not by wind. The flower is pungent; it dries well, and adds a golden glow to dull winter afternoons. This plant is small enough for small areas and tall enough to rise above its competitors.

$\times$ ¼   Color photograph, p. 44

Solidago rigida

COMMON NAMES: Stiff Goldenrod; Hard-leaved Goldenrod; Rigid Goldenrod

KIND OF PRAIRIE: Dry; Mesic

HEIGHT: 2 to 4 feet

COLOR OF FLOWER: Bright yellow-gold

FLOWERING TIME: Late August to early October: from division, the first year; from seed, the second year

SEED COLLECTION DATE: October

SEED TREATMENT: Dry stratification

PROPAGATION: Easily propagated from seed or by division. Seed sown ¼ inch deep in spring will produce transplants in one season. Divide mature plants in fall or spring. For permanent plantings, use transplants in fall or spring. Or sow unstratified seed in fall, stratified seed in spring.

COMPANION PLANTS: Big Bluestem; Leadplant; Bush Clover; Prairie-dock

COMMENT: This is a handsome plant, with good color, especially effective in isolated clumps. However, it needs competition and probably is too aggressive for small areas. A heavy seeder, it is one of the invaders in abandoned agricultural fields, particularly if they are moist. *Solidago* species have a rubbery sap from which Thomas Edison had hoped to make a rubber substitute.

$\times \frac{1}{4}$ Color photograph, p. 44

Solidago speciosa

COMMON NAMES: Showy Goldenrod; Noble Goldenrod
KIND OF PRAIRIE: Dry; Mesic
HEIGHT: 2 to 5 feet
COLOR OF FLOWER: Bright yellow-gold
FLOWERING TIME: Late August to early October: from seed, the second year
SEED COLLECTION DATE: October
SEED TREATMENT: Dry stratification
PROPAGATION: Easily propagated from seed or by division. Seed sown ¼ inch deep in spring (early June in Wisconsin) will produce transplants in one season. Divide mature plants in fall or spring. On permanent sites, use transplants in fall or spring. Or sow unstratified seed in fall, stratified seed in spring.
COMPANION PLANTS: Big Bluestem; Little Bluestem; Bush Clover; Flowering Spurge; Rough Blazingstar
COMMENT: This is the most attractive of the goldenrods, particularly in dry soils. It becomes aggressive with increased moisture. Golden flowers mix well with asters in fresh fall bouquets and dry well for winter arrangements.

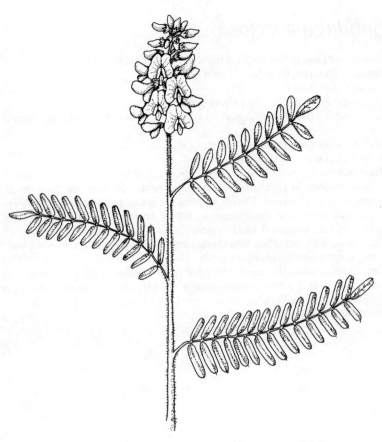

× ¼   Color photograph, p. 44

Tephrosia virginiana (A legume)

COMMON NAME: Goatsrue
KIND OF PRAIRIE: Dry
HEIGHT: 1 to 2 feet
COLOR OF FLOWER: Creamy pink two-toned flowers. (Leathery grayish foliage.)
FLOWERING TIME: June to July: from seed, the third year
SEED COLLECTION DATE: August to September
SEED TREATMENT: Scarification, inoculation, moist stratification for 10 days
PROPAGATION: Best propagated from seed. Seed pods may be very tough. If so, I use an electric drill with a sanding disk. Seed sown ½ inch deep in spring (early June in Wisconsin) will produce transplants in one season. Mature plant has long, wiry, branching taproot. Transplants more than 1 year old are very difficult to manage. On permanent sites, transplant 1-year-old roots in spring or fall. Or sow unstratified seed in fall, stratified seed in spring.
COMPANION PLANTS: Big Bluestem; Rough Blazingstar; Coreopsis; Western Sunflower
COMMENT: Colorful mature plants form attractive mounds and thrive on very dry sites. Blooms and foliage are relished by livestock. Seeds are attractive to quail. Juice was once used by Native Americans as fish poison. Roots are a source of rotenone.

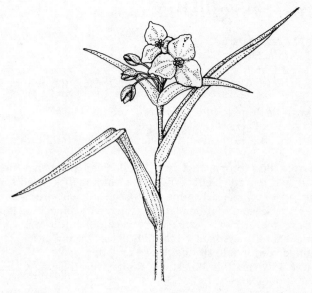

× ½   Color photograph, p. 45

Tradescantia ohiensis

COMMON NAMES: Spiderwort; Bluejacket; Widowstears; Jobstears
KIND OF PRAIRIE: Dry; Mesic; Wet
HEIGHT: 2 to 3 feet
COLOR OF FLOWER: Brilliant royal blue, sometimes white
FLOWERING TIME: June to August: from seed, the second year
SEED COLLECTION DATE: July to September
SEED TREATMENT: Moist stratification
PROPAGATION: Easily propagated from seed or by division. Seed sown ¼ inch deep in spring (June in Wisconsin) will produce transplants in one season. For permanent plantings, use transplants in fall or spring. Or sow unstratified seed in fall, stratified seed in spring.
COMPANION PLANTS: Big Bluestem; Butterfly Weed; Flowering Spurge; Junegrass; Bush Clover
COMMENT: Flowers of spiderwort, a member of the Dayflower family, unfold almost every morning. About noon petals contract and shrivel into a fluid jelly that trickles like a tear if touched. Hairy filaments suggest the spider, as do sticky threads that can be pulled from the jointed stem. The generic name honors John Tradescant, royal gardener of King Charles I, who brought the plant to England from America. Seed and plant parts are very persistent. Reportedly, the stamen hairs in certain strains mutate from blue to pink if exposed to nuclear radiation, and have been planted around a reactor site in Japan to monitor low-level radiation.

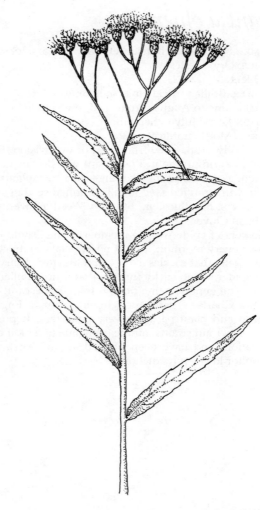

$\times$ ¼   Color photograph, p. 45

Vernonia fasciculata

COMMON NAME: Ironweed
KIND OF PRAIRIE: Mesic; Wet
HEIGHT: 2 to 5 feet
COLOR OF FLOWER: Reddish purple
FLOWERING TIME: Late July to August: from division, the first year; from seed, the second year
SEED COLLECTION DATE: October
SEED TREATMENT: Dry stratification
PROPAGATION: Easily propagated from seed or by division. To produce transplants, sow seed ¼ inch deep in spring (early June in Wisconsin) or divide 2- to 3-year-old plants; after 3 years, division is difficult. For permanent plantings, sow unstratified seed in fall, stratified seed in spring, or use transplants.
COMPANION PLANTS: New England Aster; Joe-Pye Weed; Wild Iris
COMMENT: This aggressive, bristly member of the Daisy family needs competition, and is probably too tall and coarse for small areas. "Ironweed" is for its tough, rigid stem. The generic name *Vernonia* honors William Vernon, an English botanist and explorer of the 17th century.

$\times\ \frac{1}{2}$ Color photograph, p. 45

Veronicastrum virginicum

COMMON NAMES: Culversroot; Culver's Physic

KIND OF PRAIRIE: Mesic; Wet

HEIGHT: 3 to 4 feet

COLOR OF FLOWER: White

FLOWERING TIME: Early July through mid-August: from division, the first year

SEED COLLECTION DATE: October

PROPAGATION: Best propagated by division. Seed is small and difficult to germinate, although under natural conditions it spreads reasonably well. To produce transplants, divide mature plants, and make sure each section has a bud and a root. On permanent sites, use transplants in fall or spring.

COMPANION PLANTS: Big Bluestem; Ironweed; Wild Iris; Turkscap

COMMENT: Flowers open in dense spikes that often bend. Culversroot shows off best with companion plants, and can be found along roadsides in the Northeast and the Midwest, all the way to Texas. Common name is for a Dr. Culver who used the root as a cathartic and made the plant popular. Old pharmacy handbooks listed it, suggesting the dried roots as the medication.

$\times$ 1   Color photograph, p. 45

Viola pedata

COMMON NAMES: Birdsfoot Violet; Pansy Violet

KIND OF PRAIRIE: Dry

HEIGHT: 2 to 5 inches

COLOR OF FLOWER: Pale violet; bicolor variety has dark purple upper petals.

FLOWERING TIME: May to June: from division and from seed, the second year

SEED COLLECTION DATE: July. (Seedhead explodes.)

SEED TREATMENT: Dry stratification, or fresh seed

PROPAGATION: Best propagated by division. Seed pods explode, making seeds difficult to collect. Self-seeds on open ground. To produce transplants, divide mature plants in spring or fall. On permanent sites, use transplants in fall or spring. Water heavily in fall before winter dormancy; plant is subject to freeze-out.

COMPANION PLANTS: Coreopsis; Western Sunflower; Thimbleweed; Purple Prairie Clover; Bush Clover; Lupine

COMMENT: Everyone seems to be fond of this modest, pretty plant. It depends on its colorful petaled flowers to attract insects, prefers sandy soil with good drainage and only moderate competition, and thrives in rock gardens, seaside gardens, actually any garden if all of its needs are met.

Grasses

Prairie grasses belong to the widely distributed *Gramineae* family, to which domestic lawn grasses and most cereals (wheat, barley, rye, oats, etc.) also belong. Each grass plant has a single cotyledon (first leaf), usually a hollow stem which shows no secondary thickening, and flowers with parts in threes. Prairie grasses grow in clumps; they generally are wind-pollinated.

× ½

× 12

Color photograph, p. 46

Andropogon gerardi (A warm-season grass)

COMMON NAMES: Big Bluestem; Red Hay; Turkeyfoot

KIND OF PRAIRIE: Dry; Mesic; Wet

HEIGHT: 3 to 8 feet

COLOR: Reddish seedheads in fall

FLOWERING TIME: August to September: from seed, the first or second year

SEED COLLECTION DATE: October to November

SEED TREATMENT: Dry stratification

PROPAGATION: Best propagated from seed. Mature plants are very difficult to divide. Dense root systems extend 6 to 7 feet. Seed sown ¼ inch deep in early summer (late June to early July in Wisconsin) will produce transplants in one season. On permanent sites, sow unstratified seed in fall, stratified seed in spring, or use transplants in fall or spring.

COMPANION PLANTS: Yellow Coneflower; Bergamot; Bush Clover; Rough Blazingstar; Western Sunflower; Prairiedock

COMMENT: Aggressive plants bear seed the first year under favorable conditions. On extremely dry sites they may bear seed only in wet years. Like other native grasses, their clumps will stabilize a sandblow. The attractive turkey-foot shaped seedhead is a pleasant addition to dried bouquets, especially if combined with dried *Liatris* sp.

× ½

× 12

Color photograph, p. 46

Andropogon scoparius (A warm-season grass)

COMMON NAME: Little Bluestem
KIND OF PRAIRIE: Dry; Mesic
HEIGHT: 2 to 4 feet
COLOR: Rusty-red leaves with bluish red seedhead in fall
FLOWERING TIME: August: from division, the first year; from seed if planted in May, the first year
SEED COLLECTION DATE: September to October
SEED TREATMENT: Dry stratification
PROPAGATION: Easily propagated from seed or by division. To produce transplants, sow seed ¼ inch deep in summer (late June to early July in Wisconsin), or divide mature plants in spring or fall. The older the plant, the more difficult to divide. Dense root system extends 5 to 6 feet. On permanent sites, sow unstratified seed in fall, stratified seed in spring, or use transplants in fall or spring.
COMPANION PLANTS: Leadplant; Thimbleweed; Purple Prairie Clover; Yellow Coneflower; Flowering Spurge; Butterfly Weed; Bush Clover; Junegrass.
COMMENT: This is an attractive, only moderately aggressive, grass that should be included in all prairie plantings. It forms clumps 6 to 8 inches in diameter, and is a strong seeder; often it strikes out a claim on disturbed ground downwind from a seed source. At one time it was the most abundant grass in mid-America, and still is very important in parts of Kansas and Oklahoma.

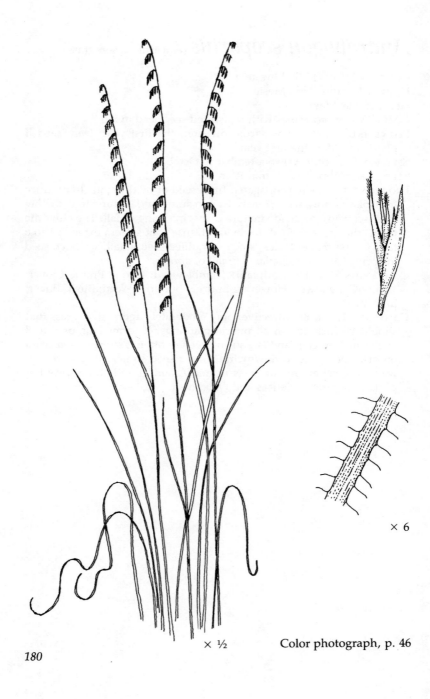

× ½

× 6

Color photograph, p. 46

Bouteloua curtipendula (A warm-season grass)

COMMON NAMES: Sideoats; Sideoats Grama

KIND OF PRAIRIE: Dry

HEIGHT: 1 to 3 feet

COLOR: Purplish seedhead in season

FLOWERING TIME: July, August, to September: from division and from seed, the first year

SEED COLLECTION DATE: Early October

SEED TREATMENT: Dry stratification

PROPAGATION: Easily propagated from seed or by division. To produce transplants, sow seed ¼ inch deep in spring (early June in Wisconsin), or divide mature plant in spring or fall. On permanent sites, sow unstratified seed in fall, stratified seed in spring, or use transplants in fall or spring.

COMPANION PLANTS: Rough Blazingstar, Leadplant; Junegrass; Flowering Spurge; Purple Prairie Clover; Little Bluestem

COMMENT: With its dense root system, this moderately aggressive plant survives in very dry soil. Small oatlike seeds are carried on one side of the stem. It is found throughout the United States east of the Rocky Mountains, and should be included in all prairie plantings.

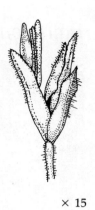

× 15

× ½

Color photograph, p. 46

Koeleria cristata (A cool-season grass)

COMMON NAME: Junegrass
KIND OF PRAIRIE: Dry
HEIGHT: 1 to 2 feet
COLOR: Silvery green seedheads
FLOWERING TIME: Late June: from division, the first year; from seed, the second year
SEED COLLECTION DATE: September to October
SEED TREATMENT: Dry stratification
PROPAGATION: Easily propagated from seed or by division. To produce transplants, divide 1- to 3-year-old plants or sow seed ¼ inch deep in early spring (mid-May in Wisconsin). It germinates best if weather is cool. Seedlings are almost invisible when first emerging. On permanent sites, sow unstratified seed in fall, stratified seed in spring, or use transplants in fall or spring.
COMPANION PLANTS: Birdsfoot Violet; Butterfly Weed; Coreopsis; Showy Goldenrod; Western Sunflower
COMMENT: This short and attractive plant has a dense and lustrous seedhead. Mature plants mix well with other prairie species.

× ½

× 12

Color photograph, p. 47

Panicum virgatum (A warm-season grass)

COMMON NAMES: Switchgrass; Panicgrass; Wild Redtop; Thatchgrass; Wobsqua Grass; Blackbent

KIND OF PRAIRIE: Dry; Mesic; Wet

HEIGHT: 3 to 5 feet

COLOR: Pale yellow leaves and seed in fall

FLOWERING TIME: August to September: from seed, the first or second year

SEED COLLECTION DATE: October

SEED TREATMENT: Dry stratification

PROPAGATION: Best propagated from seed. Division of older plants is difficult because of the tough, tangled root system. Seed sown ¼ inch deep in summer (late June to early July in Wisconsin) will produce satisfactory transplants in one season. On permanent sites, sow unstratified seed in fall, stratified seed in spring or use transplants in fall or spring.

COMPANION PLANTS: Big Bluestem; Indiangrass; Bush Clover; Yellow Coneflower; Rough Blazingstar

COMMENT: This aggressive grass grows in large clumps and needs strong competition. Probably it is too aggressive for small areas. From buffalo hunter lore we learn that some species of this grass were to be avoided when buffalo meat was cut in the field; its tiny spikes tended to stick to the meat, thence in the throats of people eating the meat. This grass has a way of creeping inside one's pants' legs, hence the origin of a few of its common names.

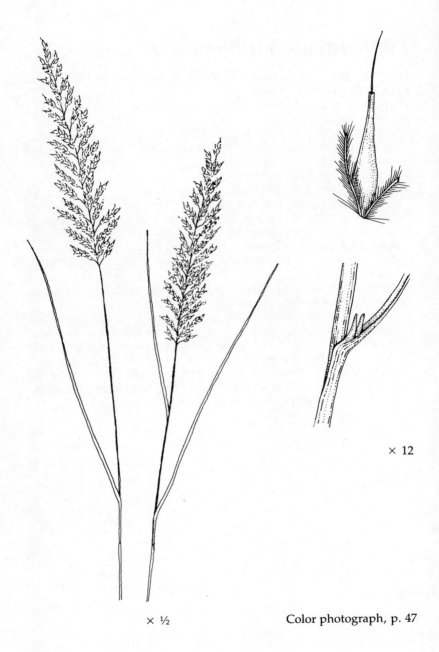

× ½

× 12

Color photograph, p. 47

Sorghastrum nutans (A warm-season grass)

COMMON NAME: Indiangrass
KIND OF PRAIRIE: Dry; Mesic
HEIGHT: 3 to 5 feet
COLOR: Bronze seedhead
FLOWERING TIME: August to September: from seed if planted in May, the first year
SEED COLLECTION DATE: October
SEED TREATMENT: Dry stratification
PROPAGATION: Best propagated from seed. Division of older plants is difficult because of the tough, tangled root system. To produce transplants, sow seed ¼ inch deep in summer (late June to early July in Wisconsin). On permanent sites, sow unstratified seed in fall, stratified seed in spring, or use transplants in fall or spring.
COMPANION PLANTS: Big Bluestem; Little Bluestem; Switchgrass; Bush Clover; Yellow Coneflower
COMMENT: This handsome grass has 6- to 10-inch plumes and glossy seedheads in fall, and is aggressive. It needs space and competition. It is found throughout the bluestem belt of the United States, primarily in parts of Kansas and Oklahoma.

× 12

× ⅓

Color photograph, p. 47

Sporobolus heterolepis (A warm-season grass)

COMMON NAME: Prairie Dropseed
KIND OF PRAIRIE: Dry; Mesic; Wet
HEIGHT: 1 to 2 feet
COLOR: Pale pinkish gold leaves and seedhead
FLOWERING TIME: August to September: from division, the first year; from seed, the second year
SEED COLLECTION DATE: October
SEED TREATMENT: Dry stratification
PROPAGATION: Propagated from seed or by division. To produce transplants, sow seed ¼ inch deep in spring (early June in Wisconsin). Seeds apparently prefer cool weather to germinate. Young plants can be divided, but old plants are difficult because of the extremely dense root system. On permanent sites, sow unstratified seed in fall, stratified seed in spring, or use transplants in fall or spring.
COMPANION PLANTS: Leadplant; Big Bluestem; Little Bluestem; Flowering Spurge; Purple Prairie Clover
COMMENT: This graceful, fine-textured grass grows in fountainlike clumps and is highly recommended for small as well as large prairie plantings. It does best on dry sites. It mixes well. Its seed is fragrant and tasty.

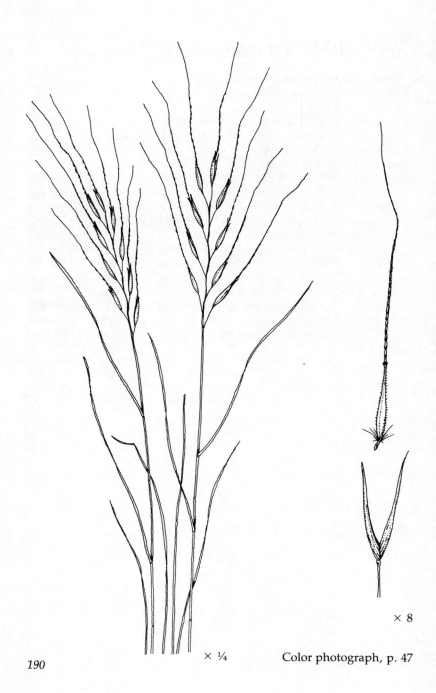

× ¼

× 8

Color photograph, p. 47

Stipa spartea (A cool-season grass)

COMMON NAME: Needlegrass
KIND OF PRAIRIE: Dry; Mesic
HEIGHT: 2 to 4 feet
COLOR: Straw-colored leaves in midsummer
FLOWERING TIME: June: from seed, the second year
SEED COLLECTION DATE: Late June to early July
SEED TREATMENT: Moist stratification, or fresh seed
PROPAGATION: Best propagated from seed. To produce transplants, sow seed ¾ inch deep in spring (mid-May in Wisconsin). Seed prefers cool weather to germinate. On permanent sites, I've had success throwing fresh collected seeds in the air, allowing them to sow themselves naturally by means of their own awns that twist with changes of humidity and force seeds into the ground. Seeds sown in this manner will germinate the following spring. Transplants can also be used in fall or spring.
COMPANION PLANTS: Prairie Dropseed; Purple Prairie Clover; Big Bluestem; Little Bluestem; Flowering Spurge; Thimbleweed; Pasque Flower; Prairie Smoke
COMMENT: Attractive on dry sites, occurring in almost solid patches, needlegrass can be found in an 18-state triangle from Colorado to Montana, east to Pennsylvania, and southwest back to Colorado. Its seeds with their long twisting awns are sharp, perhaps too sharp for plantings where there are children. The "needles" can stick in mouths, bare feet, hands, arms, anywhere.

Sedges

Sedges, grasslike plants with nearly solid stems, now belong to the *Cyperaceae* family, although they are so similar to the grasses that they once were classified as *Gramineae*. Many sedges are found in damp places; certain species of *Carex*, however, grow in dry soil. Because sedges vary widely, they are difficult to identify.

× ½

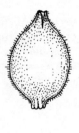

× 8

Color photograph, p. 48

194

Carex pensylvanica

COMMON NAME: Pennsylvania Sedge
KIND OF PRAIRIE: Dry
HEIGHT: 5 to 8 inches
COLOR: Pale green in spring and summer, sandy tan in fall and winter
PROPAGATION: Easily propagated by division. To produce transplants, divide mature plants in spring, making sure each section has roots and leaves. On permanent sites, use transplants in spring or fall.
COMPANION PLANTS: Pussytoes; Frostweed; False Heather; Bush Clover; Little Bluestem
COMMENT: This sedge is a fine ground cover. It spreads relentlessly by rhizomes, often forming solid circular patches in dry sandy areas. (It has been maintained as a ground cover, with the help of fertilizer, by the Moravian Church Camp at Mt. Morris, Wisconsin, for example.) Older patches often are invaded by other plants, probably because of the soil enrichment produced by the sedge.

Examples of Root Systems

One of the reasons that prairie plants are such strong survivors is the nature of their particular root systems.

Some root systems penetrate deeply into the soil. Some spread so densely that they come into contact with almost every particle of soil in the root zone. Some do both. The more shallow-rooted species of prairie plants restrict their growth to spring and fall, when moisture is plentiful.

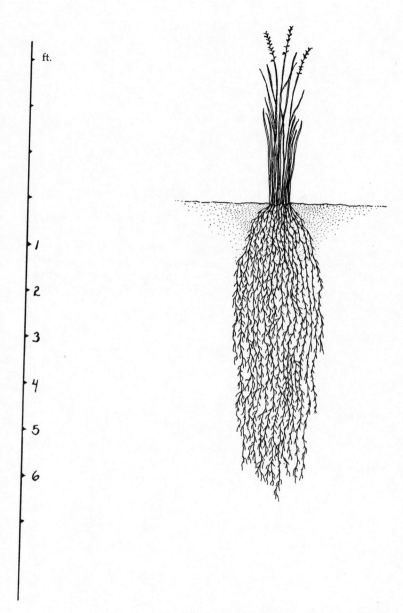

Andropogon scoparius (Little Bluestem)

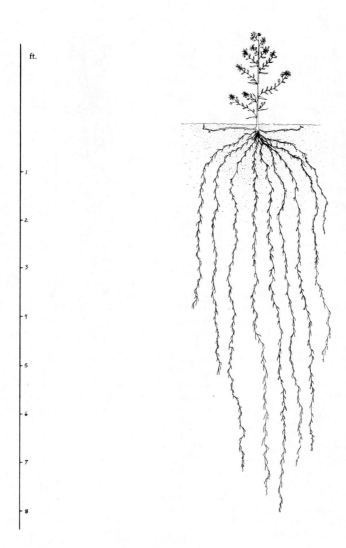

Aster ericoides (Heath Aster)

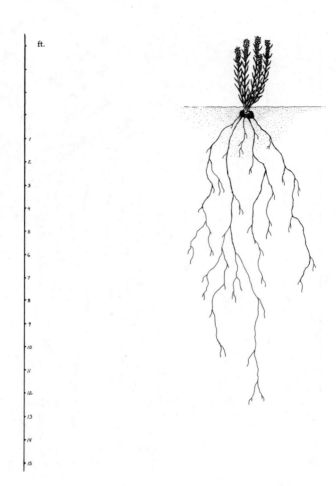

ft.

1
2
3
4
5
6
7
8
9
10
11
12
13
14
15

Liatris pycnostachya (Prairie Blazingstar)

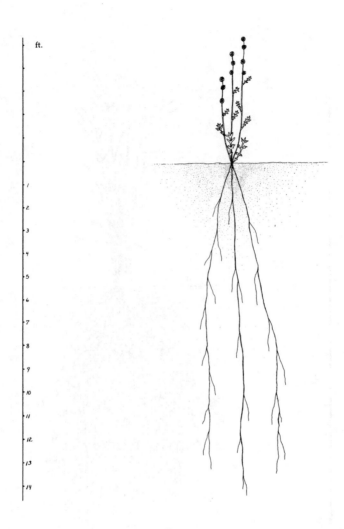

ft.

Silphium laciniatum (Compassplant)

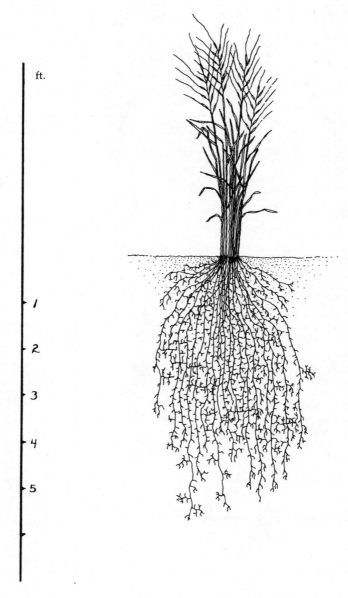

ft.

1

2

3

4

5

Stipa spartea (Needlegrass)

Prairie Plants by Habitat

Species	Dry	Mesic	Wet	Areas under 200 square feet	Areas over 200 square feet	Roadsides*
Forbs and Shrubs						
Allium cernuum		X		X	X	X
Amorpha canescens	X	X		X	X	X
Anemone cylindrica	X	X		X	X	X
Anemone patens	X	X		X	X	
Antennaria sp.	X	X		X	X	X
Aquilegia canadensis	X	X		X	X	X
Asclepias amplexicaulis	X			X	X	
Asclepias incarnata		X	X		X	X
Asclepias tuberosa	X	X		X	X	X
Aster ericoides	X	X		X	X	X
Aster novae-angliae		X	X		X	X
Aster sericeus	X	X		X	X	X
Astragalus canadensis	X				X	
Baptisia leucantha	X	X		X	X	X
Baptisia leucophaea	X	X		X	X	X
Callirhoe triangulata	X			X	X	X
Ceanothus americanus	X	X		X	X	
Coreopsis palmata	X	X		X	X	X
Delphinium virescens	X	X		X	X	
Dodecatheon meadia	X	X	X	X	X	
Echinacea pallida	X	X		X	X	X
Echinacea purpurea	X			X	X	X
Eryngium yuccifolium	X	X			X	
Euphorbia corollata	X	X		X	X	X
Filipendula rubra		X	X	X	X	
Gentiana andrewsii		X	X	X	X	
Geum triflorum	X	X		X	X	X
Helianthus occidentalis	X	X		X	X	X
Heuchera richardsonii	X	X	X	X	X	
Hudsonia tomentosa	X			(Sandblows)		
Iris shrevei		X	X	X	X	X
Lespedeza capitata	X	X		X	X	
Liatris aspera	X	X		X	X	X
Liatris cylindracea	X			X	X	X

* Only the most showy and competitive plants are listed.

Species	Dry	Mesic	Wet	Areas under 200 square feet	Areas over 200 square feet	Roadsides*
Forbs and Shrubs (cont.)						
Liatris pycnostachya		X	X	X	X	X
Lilium superbum		X	X	X	X	X
Lithospermum croceum	X	X		X	X	X
Lupinus perennis	X	X		X	X	X
Monarda fistulosa	X	X	X	X	X	X
Monarda punctata	X				X	X
Oenothera biennis	X	X			X	
Petalostemum candidum	X	X		X	X	
Petalostemum purpureum	X	X		X	X	X
Phlox pilosa	X	X	X	X	X	
Psoralea esculenta	X			X	X	
Ranunculus rhomboideus	X			X	X	X
Ratibida pinnata	X	X	X		X	X
Rosa sp.	X	X		X	X	X
Rudbeckia hirta	X	X	X	X	X	X
Silphium laciniatum	X	X			X	X
Silphium perfoliatum		X	X	X	X	X
Silphium terebinthinaceum		X	X		X	X
Sisyrinchium campestre	X			X	X	X
Solidago nemoralis	X			X	X	X
Solidago rigida	X	X		X	X	X
Solidago speciosa	X	X		X	X	X
Tephrosia virginiana	X			X	X	X
Tradescantia ohiensis	X	X	X	X	X	X
Vernonia fasciculata		X	X		X	
Veronicastrum virginicum		X	X	X	X	X
Viola pedata	X			X	X	X
Grasses						
Andropogon gerardi	X	X	X	X		
Andropogon scoparius	X	X		X	X	X
Bouteloua curtipendula	X			X	X	X
Koeleria cristata	X			X	X	
Panicum virgatum	X	X	X		X	X
Sorghastrum nutans	X	X			X	
Sporobolus heterolepis	X	X	X	X	X	X
Stipa spartea	X	X			X	
Sedge						
Carex pensylvanica	X			X	X	X

Prairie Plants by Color and Flowering Time

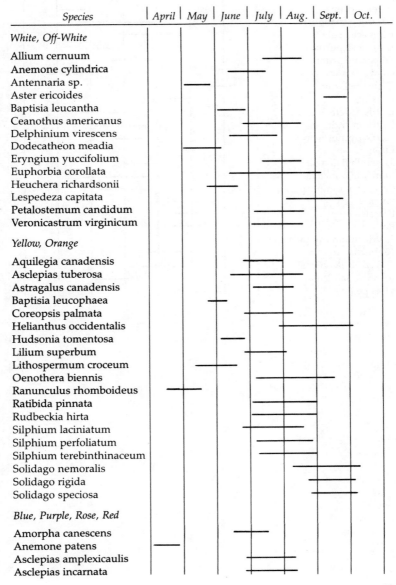

Species	April	May	June	July	Aug.	Sept.	Oct.

White, Off-White

Allium cernuum
Anemone cylindrica
Antennaria sp.
Aster ericoides
Baptisia leucantha
Ceanothus americanus
Delphinium virescens
Dodecatheon meadia
Eryngium yuccifolium
Euphorbia corollata
Heuchera richardsonii
Lespedeza capitata
Petalostemum candidum
Veronicastrum virginicum

Yellow, Orange

Aquilegia canadensis
Asclepias tuberosa
Astragalus canadensis
Baptisia leucophaea
Coreopsis palmata
Helianthus occidentalis
Hudsonia tomentosa
Lilium superbum
Lithospermum croceum
Oenothera biennis
Ranunculus rhomboideus
Ratibida pinnata
Rudbeckia hirta
Silphium laciniatum
Silphium perfoliatum
Silphium terebinthinaceum
Solidago nemoralis
Solidago rigida
Solidago speciosa

Blue, Purple, Rose, Red

Amorpha canescens
Anemone patens
Asclepias amplexicaulis
Asclepias incarnata

Species	April	May	June	July	Aug.	Sept.	Oct.
Aster novae-angliae						■	■
Aster sericeus						■	
Callirhoe triangulata			■	■	■		
Echinacea pallida			■	■			
Echinacea purpurea				■	■		
Filipendula rubra				■			
Gentiana andrewsii						■	■
Geum triflorum	■	■					
Iris shrevei		■	■				
Liatris aspera					■		
Liatris cylindracea				■			
Liatris pycnostachya				■	■		
Lupinus perennis		■					
Monarda fistulosa				■	■		
Monarda punctata				■	■	■	
Petalostemum purpureum				■	■		
Phlox pilosa		■	■				
Psoralea esculenta		■					
Rosa sp.		■	■				
Sisyrinchium campestre	■	■					
Tephrosia virginiana			■				
Tradescantia ohiensis		■	■	■			
Vernonia fasciculata					■		
Viola pedata	■	■					

Number of Seeds per Pound of Selected Species

Species	Seeds per pound	
Forbs		
Baptisia leucophaea	31,752 S	
Ceanothus americanus	65,772 S	
Coreopsis palmata	75,526 S	371,000 H
Dodecatheon meadia	1,224,720 S	
Echinacea pallida	68,040 S	
Eryngium yuccifolium	127,008 S	
Helianthus occidentalis	149,688 S	
Lespedeza capitata	113,400 S	51,250 H
Liatris aspera	136,080 S	122,000 H
Lupinus perennis	20,000 P	153,750 H
Monarda fistulosa	680,000 S	153,750 H
Phlox pilosa	163,296 S	
Ratibida pinnata	362,880 S	337,500 H
Rudbeckia hirta	1,587,600 S	482,150 H
Silphium laciniatum	12,700 S	
Solidago rigida	249,480 S	282,600 H
Veronicastrum virginicum	2,721,600 S	
Grasses		
Andropogon gerardi	165,000 W	
Andropogon scoparius	260,000 W	
Bouteloua curtipendula	191,000 W	
Panicum virgatum	389,000 W	
Sorghastrum nutans	175,000 W	272,160 S
Sporobolus heterolepis	263,088 S	
Stipa spartea	13,154 S	

H: Information compiled by Marlene Halinar, UW graduate student, Department of Landscape Architecture.

P: Information from J. R. Smith, Prairie Nursery, Westfield, Wisconsin.

W: Information from Jim Wilson, Wilson Seed Farms, Polk, Nebraska.

S: Information compiled by Jerry Schwarzmeier, Waukesha County botanist.

Cost Comparison Chart
(Prepared by Prairie Restorations, Inc., Wayzata, MN)

	Native		*Bluegrass*
	INITIAL COST PER ACRE		
Prairie grass seed and seedlings	$ 290	Sodding bluegrass ($.70/sq. yd.)	$3400
Wildflowers (2000 seedlings, plus planting)	2500		
Site preparation	400	Site preparation	500
Watering and 2 mowings 1st year	90	Watering 1st year	100
		Mowing 1st year	160
TOTAL/ACRE*	$3280	TOTAL/ACRE	$4160
	ANNUAL UPKEEP PER ACRE		
Mowing or burning (including cost of equipment rental)	$100	Mowing	$200
		Watering	100
		Fertilizing	80
		Aerifying, leaf removal, top dressing	150
		Equipment maintenance, depreciation	200
TOTAL/ACRE	$100	TOTAL/ACRE	$730

*General estimate based on 5- to 10-acre project, 2000 first-year wildflower seedlings @ $.80 each average cost plus $.45 for planting. Wildflower planting may vary from 500 to 5000 seedlings per acre depending on desired effect and cost. Site preparation will vary widely from site to site.

Sources of Prairie, Woodland, and Wetland Plants and Seeds

Dutch Mt Nursery
Rt. 1, 7984 N. 48th St.
Augusta, MI 49012
Ferndale Nursery
Askov, MN 55704
Game Food Nurseries
Oshkosh, WI 54020
Harry E. Saier
Dimondale, MI 48821
High Meadow Farm
Rt. 1, Box 215
Mt. Horeb, WI 53572
Lafayette Home Nursery
Lafayette, IL 63673
Little Valley Farm
Rt. 1, Box 286
Richland Center, WI 53581
Lounsberry Gardens
Box 135
Oakford, IL 62673
Midwest Wildflowers
Box 64
Rockton, IL 62673
Natural Habitats Nursery
4818 Terminal Rd.
McFarland, WI 53558
Oscar H. Will Co.
Bismarck, ND 58500

Orchid Gardens
Rt. 1
Grand Rapids, MN 55744
The Potting Shed
Box 11638
Milwaukee, WI 53211
Prairie Associates
6328 Piping Rock Rd.
Madison, WI 53711
Prairie Gem Ranch
Smithwick, SD 57782
Prairie Nursery
Box 116
Westfield, WI 53964
Prairie Restoration
990 Old Long Lake Rd.
Wayzata, MN 55391
Prairie Ridge Nursery
Rt. 2, Overland Rd.
Mount Horeb, WI 53572
Wildlife Nurseries
Box 399
Oshkosh, WI 54901
Windrift Prairie Nursery
Rt. 2
Oregon, IL 61061
Woodlands Acres Nursery
Rt. 2
Crivitz, WI 54114

C.A. Cruickshank, Ltd.
1015 Mount Pleasant Rd.
Toronto, Ontario 315
Canada
Clyde Robin Seed Co., Inc.
Box 2855
Castro Valley, CA 94546
Exeter Wildflower Gardens
Box 510
Exeter, NH 03833

Keith Somers
10 Tillson Ave.
Tillsonburg, Ontario
Canada
Leslie's Wildflower Nursery
30 Summer St.
Methuen, MA 01844
Miles W. Fry & Sons Nursery
Rt. 3
Ephrata, PA 17522

Gardenside Nursery
　Shelburne, VT 05482
Gardens of the Blue Ridge
　Box 10
　Pineola, NC 28662
Griffey's Nursery
　Rt. 3, Box 17A
　Marshall, NC 28753

Putney Nursery, Inc.
　Putney, VT 05341
Vicks Wild Flower Gardens
　Box 115
　Gladwyne, PA 19035

Note: This is not a complete list. Native-species nurseries are continually popping up, and many conventional nurseries list native flowers, shrubs, and trees. State departments of natural resources, botanical gardens, arboretums, nursery associations, landscape architects, and the U.S. Department of Agriculture, Washington, D.C., should be able to supply further information. In addition, the Soil Conservation Society of America, 7515 Northeast Ankeny Rd., Ankeny, IA 50021, has a booklet, "Sources of Native Seeds and Plants," in which sources throughout the United States are listed ($2.00 postpaid).

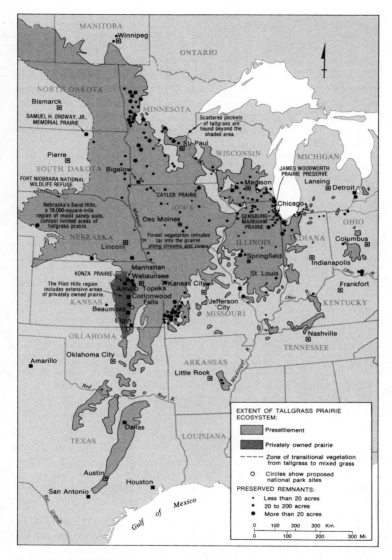

Locations of prairies. (Map redrawn by the University of Wisconsin-Madison Cartographic Laboratory from "Remnants of the once vast tallgrass prairie," *National Geographic Magazine* 157, no. 1 [January 1980]: 43, by permission of the National Geographic Society.)

Suggested Reading

Britton, Nathanial and Brown, Addison. *An Illustrated Flora of the Northern United States, Canada and the British Possessions.* 3 vols. New York: Charles Scribner and Sons, 1913. Reprinted. New York: Dover Publications, Inc., 1970.

Costello, David F. *The Prairie World.* New York: Thomas Y. Crowell Co., 1969.
Covers plants and animals of the prairie and their effects on each other. Many excellent photos.

Cottam, Grant. "Management: Our First 45 Years." *Arboretum News* 28 (Winter, 1979).
A brief history of the University of Wisconsin Arboretum, Madison, WI. Informative.

Courtenay, Booth, and Zimmerman, James H. *Wild Flowers and Weeds.* New York: Van Nostrand Reinhold Co., 1976.
Excellent field guide with colored photos.

Crowns, Byron. *Wisconsin Through 5 Billion Years of Change.* Madison, WI: Wisconsin Earth Science Center, 1976.
Geological history of Wisconsin.

Curtis, John T. *Vegetation of Wisconsin.* Madison, WI: University of Wisconsin Press, 1959.
Excellent description of plant communities.

Duncan, Patricia. *Tallgrass Prairies: The Inland Sea.* Kansas City, MO: Lowell Press, 1978.
A factual, philosophic overview of the tallgrass prairie, with emphasis on Kansas.

Fassett, Norman C., 4th ed., revised and enlarged by Olive S. Thomson. *Spring Flora of Wisconsin.* Madison, WI: University of Wisconsin Press, 1976.
A fine identification guide, if you know plant structure.

Fassett, Norman C. *Grasses of Wisconsin.* Madison, WI: University of Wisconsin Press 1951.
Fine guide, with drawings and range maps.

Fiedler, Mildred. *Plant Medicine and Folklore.* New York: Winchester Press, 1975.
Entertaining and informative, with black and white photos and illustrations.

Germaine, Clifford E., Tans, William E., and Read, Robert H. *Wisconsin Scientific Areas.* Technical Bulletin 102. Madison, WI: Wisconsin Department of Natural Resources, 1977.
An informative study of the scientific areas in Wisconsin.

Hammerstrom, Frederick and Frances, and Matson, Oswald E. *Sharptails into the Shadows.* Madison, WI: Game Management Division of Wisconsin Conservation Department, 1952.
History of tree-planting in the barrens and subsequent disappearance of sharp-tailed grouse.

Kenfield, Warren. *The Wild Gardener in the Wild Landscape*. New York: Hafner Press, 1966.

Good ideas, but too dependent on herbicides. Entertaining reading.

Klimas, John, and Cunningham, James. *Wildflowers of Eastern America*. New York: Alfred A. Knopf, Inc., 1974.

A field guide with 300 color photos, plus folklore and history.

Korling, Torkel. *The Prairie Swell and Swale*. Dundee, IL: T. Korling, 1972.

Outstanding color photos; includes a short history of Midwest prairies by Robert Betz.

Leopold, Aldo. *A Sand County Almanac*. New York: Oxford University Press, 1949.

Thoughts, feelings, and challenges of a pioneer naturalist.

Minnich, Jerry. *Wisconsin Garden Guide*. Madison, WI: Wisconsin House, 1975.

Excellent on general gardening in Wisconsin, includes information on weather, insects, diseases, etc., helpful to the prairie gardener.

Moldenke, Harold. *American Wildflowers*. New York: D. Van Nostrand, Inc., Viking Press, 1949.

Copiously illustrated book of the most showy plants in North America.

Morrison, Darrel. "Notes on Design and Establishment of Prairies." Madison, WI: Darrel Morrison, University of Wisconsin—Madison Department of Landscaping, 1979.

Helpful information on seeding rates and what to expect of prairie plants.

Nichols, Stan, and Entine, Lynn. *The Prairie Primer*. Madison, WI: University of Wisconsin Extension, 1976.

Forty pages of information on prairie plants; illustrated.

Northern, Henry and Rebecca. *Ingenious Kingdom*. Englewood Cliffs, NJ: Prentice-Hall, Inc., 1970.

Enthusiastic study of plant "behavior."

Orr, Robert and Margaret. *Wildflowers of Western America*. New York: Alfred A. Knopf, Inc., 1974.

A field guide with color photos, descriptions, and comments.

Oosting, Henry. *Plant Communities*. San Francisco: Freeman, Cooper, and Co., 1956.

An introduction to plant ecology. Solid, technical information.

Paull, Rachel and Richard. *Geology of Wisconsin and Upper Michigan*. Dubuque, IA: Kendall/Hunt, 1977.

Peterson, Roger Tory. *Field Guide to Wildflowers*. Boston: Houghton Mifflin Co., 1968.

A classic.

Phillips Petroleum Co. *Native Grasses, Legumes and Forbs*. Bartlesville, OK, 1955, 1959.

Prairie plants from the viewpoint of the stockman. Illustrated.

Rickett, H. W. *Wild Flowers of the U.S. Northeastern States*. New York: McGraw-Hill Book Co., Inc., 1965.

Especially valuable for its large color photographs.

Robin, Clyde. *Catalog*. Castro Valley, CA: Clyde Robin Seed Co., Inc.: 1970–72.

Catalog of a worldwide plant collector with how-to information included.

Rock, Harold W. *Prairie Propagation Handbook*. Milwaukee, WI: Milwaukee Park System, 1974.

A must for every prairie plant grower; includes several hundred species.

Sears, P. B. *Lands Beyond the Forest*. Englewood Cliffs, NJ: Prentice-Hall, Inc., 1969.

Discusses relationships between mankind and grasslands.

Smith, A. W. *A Gardener's Book of Plant Names*. New York: Harper and Row, 1963.

Information about origins and meanings of plant names.

Sperka, Marie. *Growing Wildflowers*. New York: Harper and Row, 1969.

Excellent information about growing woodland and prairie plants by a gardener who has done it.

Stoekler, J. H. *Forest Nursery Practice in the Lake States*. Agriculture Handbook 110. Washington, D.C.: Government Printing Office, 1957.

Swink, Floyd. *Plants of the Chicago Region*. Lisle, IL: Morton Arboretum, 1974.

An alphabetical listing, including habitats and companion plants.

U.S. Department of Agriculture. *Grass*. 1948 Yearbook of Agriculture. Washington, D.C.: Government Printing Office, 1948.

Comprehensive book on grasses, including some prairie grasses.

U.S. Department of Agriculture. *Seeds*. 1961 Yearbook of Agriculture. Washington, D.C.: Government Printing Office, 1961.

Filled with information about seeds of all kinds.

Weaver, John E. *North American Prairie*. Richmond, VA: Johnson Publishing Co., 1954.

A classic text, easy to read; includes illustrations of plant roots.

Weaver, John E. and Clements, F. E. *Plant Ecology*. New York: McGraw-Hill Book Co., Inc., 1929, 1938.

A comprehensive textbook and guide.

214

Index

Cupplant, 152–53
Cutting and raking, 32

Darkyhead. *See* Blackeyed Susan
Delphinium virescens, 88–89; color photograph, 36. *See also* Prairie Larkspur
Devil's Bite. *See* Rough Blazingstar
Diseases: in greenhouse, 18; in general, 23
Division of plants, 21–22
Dodecatheon meadia, 90–91; color photograph, 36. *See also* Shootingstar
Dotted Mint, 27, 29, 130–31
Downy Phlox. *See* Prairie Phlox
Drainage problems, 10–11
Dwarf Blazingstar, 26, 118–19
Dwarf Buttercup, 142–43

Easter Flower. *See* Pasque Flower
Echinacea pallida, 92–93; color photograph, 37
Echinacea purpurea, 94–95; color photograph, 37. *See also* Purple Coneflower
Elephant Ear. *See* Prairiedock
Endangered species, 12
English Bull's-eye. *See* Blackeyed Susan
Eryngium yuccifolium, 96–97; color photograph, 37
Euphorbia corollata, 98–99; color photograph, 37
Evening Primrose, 132–33

False Heather, 110–11
Fertility, 10, 18, 23, 30
Fertilizer, 20, 29, 30
Fever Plant, 132–33
Filipendula rubra, 100–101; color photograph, 37
Flats: use of, 18–19
Flowering Spurge, 13, 27, 29, 98–99
Forbs, 27, 31
Frost heaving, 21

Gayfeather, 120–21. *See also* Rough Blazingstar; Dwarf Blazingstar
Gentiana andrewsii, 102–3; color photograph, 38. *See also* Bottle Gentian
Germination, 15–16, 19
Geum triflorum, 104–5; color photograph, 38. *See also* Prairie Smoke
Goatsrue, 164–65
Grandpa's Whiskers. *See* Prairie Smoke
Grasses, 20, 25, 26, 27, 30, 31
Grass-forb ratio, 24
Gray Goldenrod, 158–59
Grayheaded Coneflower. *See* Yellow Coneflower
Greenhouse: uses of, 17–19
Gumweed. *See* Compassplant

Hairy Puccoon, 124–25
Hard-leaved Goldenrod, 160–61
Heath Aster, 70–71
Heeling bed: use of, 21
Helianthus occidentalis, 106–7; color photograph, 38
Herbicides, 10, 30
Heuchera richardsonii, 108–9; color photograph, 38. *See also* Alumroot
Horsemint. *See* Bergamot; Dotted Mint
Hudsonia tomentosa, 110–11; color photograph, 39

Indianchief. *See* Shootingstar
Indian Cup, 152–53
Indiangrass, 19, 26, 186–87
Indian Posy. *See* Butterfly Weed
Inoculant: how to add, 15; need for, 15; where to purchase, 15
Insect control, 23
Insecticides, 23
Iris shrevei, 112–13; color photograph, 39
Ironweed, 168–69
Irrigation. *See* Watering

Jobstears. *See* Spiderwort
Junegrass, 26, 29, 182–83

King's Cure-all, 132–33
Koeleria cristata, 182–83; color photograph, 46. *See also* Junegrass

Ladys-leek, 52–53
Large areas: preparation of, 9–10; sowing seed on, 26–27; using transplants on, 28; weed control of, 30; maintenance of, 30–32
Larksheel. *See* Prairie Larkspur
Leadplant, 7, 16, 19, 21, 26, 54–55
Legumes, 15, 25, 27, 29, 30, 79, 81, 115, 127, 135, 137, 141, 165
Lespedeza capitata, 114–15; color photograph, 39. *See also* Bush Clover
Liatris aspera, 13, 20, 22, 116–17; color photograph, 39. *See also* Rough Blazingstar
Liatris cylindracea, 13, 20, 22, 118–19; color photograph, 40. *See also* Dwarf Blazingstar
Liatris pycnostachya, 13, 20, 22, 120–21; color photograph, 40
Lilium superbum, 122–23; color photograph, 40
Lithospermum croceum, 124–25; color photograph, 40
Little Bluestem, 13, 19, 22, 25, 26, 29, 30–31, 178–79
Little Rattlepod, 76–77
Lupine, 5–6, 13, 19, 30, 126–27
Lupinus perennis, 126–27; color photograph, 40. *See also* Lupine

Marsh Milkweed, 13, 66–67
Meadow Rose. *See* Prairie Rose
Michaelmas Daisy, 70–71
Milk Ipecac. *See* Flowering Spurge
Milk-vetch, 76–77
Monarda fistulosa, 128–29; color photograph, 40
Monarda punctata, 130–31; color photograph, 41. *See also* Dotted Mint
Mowing: as weed control measure, 30
Mulching: to maintain moisture, 20; to prevent frost heaving, 21

Needlegrass, 26, 190–91
New England Aster, 72–73
New Jersey Tea, 6, 23, 84–85
Night Willow Herb, 132–33
Noble Goldenrod, 162–63
Nodding Pink Onion, 52–53
Nurse crop, 28

Oats, 28
Oenothera biennis, 132–33; color photograph, 41
Orange Milkweed. *See* Butterfly Weed
Orange Root. *See* Butterfly Weed
Orange Swallowwort. *See* Butterfly Weed

Pale Purple Coneflower, 92–93
Panicgrass. *See* Switchgrass
Panicum virgatum, 184–85; color photograph, 47. *See also* Switchgrass
Pansy Violet. *See* Birdsfoot Violet
Pasque Flower, 13, 18, 20, 23, 58–59
Pasture Rose. *See* Prairie Rose
Pennsylvania Sedge, 194–95
Persistence of prairie plants, 6–7
Pests, 22–23
Petalostemum candidum, 134–35; color photograph, 41. *See also* White Prairie Clover
Petalostemum purpureum, 136–37; color photograph, 41. *See also* Purple Prairie Clover
Phlox pilosa, 138–39; color photograph, 42. *See also* Prairie Phlox
Pilotweed. *See* Compassplant
Plastic: as weed control measure, 9–10
Pleurisy Root. *See* Butterfly Weed
Pollination, 22, 51
Poorland Daisy. *See* Blackeyed Susan
Poppy Mallow, 18, 82–83
Prairie Blazingstar, 120–21
Prairie Blue-eyed Grass, 156–57
Prairie Buttercup, 142–43
Prairie Coneflower. *See* Yellow Coneflower
Prairie Crowfoot, 142–43

DESIGNED BY IRVING PERKINS ASSOCIATES
COMPOSED BY GRAPHIC COMPOSITION, INC.
ATHENS, GEORGIA
MANUFACTURED BY THOMSON SHORE, INC.
DEXTER, MICHIGAN
TEXT AND DISPLAY LINES ARE SET IN PALATINO

Library of Congress Cataloging in Publication Data
Smith, J   Robert, 1914–
The prairie garden.
Bibliography: p.
Includes index.
1. Prairie gardening. 2. Prairie flora.
I. Smith, Beatrice S., joint author.
II. Title
SB434.3.S64   635.9′5   80-5116
ISBN 0-299-08300-4
ISBN 0-299-08304-7 (pbk.)